Hack Your Depression

Kas Thomas

Table of Contents

Introduction

> It was the self, the purpose and essence of which I sought to learn. It was the self, I wanted to free myself from, which I sought to overcome. But I was not able to overcome it, could only deceive it, could only flee from it, only hide from it. Truly, no thing in this world has kept my thoughts thus busy, as this my very own self, this mystery of me being alive, of me being one and being separated and isolated from all others, of me being Siddhartha! And there is no thing in this world I know less about than about me, about Siddhartha!
>
> *Siddhartha*, Hermann Hesse

Maybe you've noticed that no matter where you go in this life, whether it's to a geographical destination or some other kind of destination, you rarely, if ever, get where you're going in a straight line. Invariably, there are twists, turns, detours, setbacks, switchbacks, course corrections, obstacles, distractions, diversions, things you didn't plan on. But eventually you wind up at the destination. Sometimes. Often enough.

This is an important point to bear in mind, regarding recovery from a mental disorder. If you expect to make straight-line progress from Point A to Point B, you'll be disappointed. But if you make appreciable (if only small) amounts of progress, on an often-enough basis, you'll get where you're going. Expect some zigs; expect some zags. It's the nature of progress.

I feel a certain amount of hesitancy in writing what comes next, to tell you the truth. I'm not a therapist. I have no formal training in psychology (beyond two introductory psych courses and a "psycho-biology" lab, in college). I'm not sure I can articulate what I want to say, in a way that will be satisfying; and I don't want to disappoint. I've been disappointed many times, in therapy. I know what that feels like.

Also, I can't claim to be 100% recovered from my depression (technically dysthymia at this point), and I don't want to give the impression that I'm in possession of some "special knowledge" that has helped me achieve a spectacular recovery that hasn't happened. I've gotten significantly better; that much, I can tell you with a straight face. I'm no longer bipolar (and haven't been since September 2012). But I still have work to do.

More than that, I'm disdainful of quick fixes of the "10 Things You Need to Know" type, and I *loathe* homespun homilies of the "things could always be worse" variety.

And finally, I know that what works for me won't necessarily work for you. Every person's situation is different. Every person's mental condition is different. One size never fits all, in this business.

I'm going to list some "learnings," in this slim volume, that I've taken from therapy (and from life) over the years. They're subject to the disclaimers listed above. Use these tips in good health *and* at your own risk. This book is not a substitute for therapy and comes with no guarantees. What I recommend, whenever you encounter a compilation of tips like the ones you'll find in this book, is that you do what I do: *Take from it what you can, discard the rest.* If something seems worthwhile, profit from it. If something *doesn't* seem worthwhile, shrug it off—and move on.

Before continuing, I have to issue one more caution. It's been my observation (and I feel certain many therapists will back me up on this) that some people *aren't ready* to get better. Not everyone can be helped by therapy, or by a 12-step program, or by an intervention. If you've met an alcoholic who's still drinking, you know what I'm talking about. That person isn't ready to get better. He or she may *want* to get better; he or she may *say* "I want to get better!"; but an alcoholic who's still drinking simply "isn't there yet." Quite often, unfortunately, hard-core addicts need to hit rock bottom before they realize, finally, they truly *want* and *need* to get better. This isn't always the case, but it happens often enough.

You have to *want* to get better, yes; but you also have to be *ready* to get better. That means you have to be ready for *change*. Some people aren't open to that. They just aren't ready.

It's possible to reach a point in your depression where you are beyond the help of any therapist, beyond "talk therapy"; only suicide seems like an option. When you've reached that point, you need an intervention. In many parts of the U.S., you can dial 2-1-1 for mental health emergencies. Otherwise, call (or have a friend call) the Suicide Prevention Hotline at 1 (800) 273-8255. Or dial 9-1-1.

If you need an intervention, don't feel bad. Don't beat yourself up over it. I was in "the mental ward" twice (I talk about it later in this book) and it was the best thing that ever happened to me.

If you haven't tried "talk therapy," it's definitely worth trying, although it's not easy to find the right therapist. The most important advice I can give you here is: Don't look for a buddy—someone who's easy to talk to in a *hi-how-are-you* kind of way. Good rapport isn't really what you're looking for in a therapist and can actually hinder therapy. You want someone who can *cut through* the chit-chat and get down to business. If you settle for a therapist who "makes you comfortable," you're making a mistake. You'll settle into a comfort zone. You'll talk a lot, but no healing will take place. How can it, if you insist on staying in a comfort zone?

Therapy is about going to the dark places you don't want to go to, talking about issues that are difficult, scary, emotional. You need a special kind of person for that, someone you feel safe with but who won't let you stay in your comfort zone—a tour guide of the soul. That's not so easy to find.

When therapy works, people sometimes get worse before they get better. Prepare yourself for that eventuality. You may go into therapy and find that the things you end up talking about re-traumatize you, to an extent. That's not uncommon, and it's not necessarily a bad thing. Bringing ugly stuff up to the surface, where you can shine the light of reason on it, can be discomfiting. ("People with PTSD often have more bad dreams right after starting therapy," a Ph.D. Psychologist told me recently.) But getting the ugly stuff to come out, where it can be dealt with, is often a necessary step in getting better.

Talk therapy doesn't always work—and when it works, it doesn't always work right away. Every person's case is different. You need to be patient. But you also need to keep trying different therapists until you get the one who's right for you. If you're not seeing benefits after six or eight sessions, ask yourself if maybe you shouldn't branch out and try someone else, rather than go another eight sessions with the same person. (I mention eight as an example. *You* decide what the right number of sessions is. Certainly, if you haven't seen benefit after eight sessions, there's reason for concern.)

I want to reemphasize the point I made at the beginning, which was: Don't expect straight-line progress. Don't set the bar too high. Getting better is a matter of taking many small steps, some of which will be in the wrong direction. That's fine. That's how life is. The goal is to make progress *over time,* not score a home run in your first at-bat. You have to play 162 games to get to post-season playoffs in baseball. Even the best team in baseball is not going to win all 162 games. It doesn't happen that way. Progress is incremental, intermittent.

The parts of this book can be read in any order. But you might want to skip ahead to the first Appendix ("Mind over Matter") and start there. That Appendix is quite important, because it talks about the formidable, often mysterious, never to be underestimated healing powers of the mind. I included that section as a reminder that you already carry within you a truly vast capacity for healing. Sometimes the first step in healing is to believe healing is possible. It helps to have a reminder of what the mind is capable of. I hope the "Mind over Matter" discussion convinces you (as it did me, while I was researching and writing it) that the mind is awesomely powerful, a fantastic reservoir of healing energy.

The second Appendix ("Is Mental Illness Biological?") is also important, because whether or not you believe mental illnesses are biological, it's been shown, through a variety of sociological experiments, that biological theories of "chemical imbalance," and theories involving *genetic* causes for mental disorders (which are not at all well proven, in my opinion), actually foster more pessimistic expectations for recovery. Biological theories reduce blame-oriented stigma but increase other forms of prejudice. They can actually foster a negative attitude toward prognosis and recovery. It's important not to fall into that trap.

I wouldn't write a book like this if I didn't feel recovery from depression (and other mental disorders) is possible. But I'm no Pollyanna. I'm a realist, and a bit of a cynic, actually, when it comes to many therapeutic options. The success rate of current therapeutic options for depression is, on the whole, not terribly good. Drugs work for between 30% and 60% of patients (depending on the disorder), although placebos work almost as well. Even when drugs do work, relapse is common. Electroconvulsive therapy (ECT) has been vastly oversold and is based on extremely shoddy research, something I talk about in detail in the third Appendix of this book. (Please read that Appendix before trying, or letting anyone you know try, shock therapy.) "Talk therapy" works for many people (indeed, it's well proven), but certain modalities, like Cognitive Behavioral Therapy (CBT), have been grossly oversold on the basis of research that can only be described as disappointingly substandard. Mind you, I think CBT does have useful things to teach. Many people have benefited from it. But many studies have shown that the cognitive "special ingredients" of CBT can be omitted without reducing CBT's effectiveness.[1] Hence, the theoretical basis of CBT is on shaky ground.

The tips offered in this book draw from a variety of sources. Many are learnings derived from my own years in therapy. Some are life lessons I've figured out on my own. Some were inspired by the teachings in certain books I've found useful, such as Steve Chandler's *100 Ways to Motivate Yourself* (Career Books, 2004). A few of the tips are (arguably) Zen-like, although I am not a practitioner of Zen, per se.

Since I'm a realist and a skeptic who doesn't buy into any particular psychological theory or therapeutic school of thought, someone who rejects simplistic homespun advice of the "happiness is a choice" variety (and doesn't put much stock in affirmations or other easy pop-psych solutions), you should know that the tips in this book come from a place of hard-core, brutal reality. Be prepared for that. Some of the tips may sound a bit *too* brutally honest. I stand by them, my main justification being: *This is what works for me*. The tips may or may not work for you. Only know, it took me *years*—and thousands of dollars in therapy—to find these things out. My sincere hope is that you find these learnings worthwhile. May you use them to great and lasting personal benefit.

I've rarely been one to spindle, dog-ear, write in, or otherwise mutilate books, because I was raised to respect books as sacred objects. As I've grown older, though, I've come to see the wisdom of violating this rule for certain books—books with content too valuable *not* to underline, dog-ear, etc. My fondest secret wish (are you ready?) is that you'll buy a fistful of colored markers and highlight the crap out of *this* book, dog-earing its pages mercilessly, underlining favorite passages, putting stars in the margins, and so on, until the book is thoroughly, irrevocably yours and yours alone. So please: Mark it up. Circle things. Underline. Go crazy. It's just a book. Make it yours.

---

1   See Longmore, R.J. & Worrell, M. (2007), "Do we need to challenge thoughts in cognitive behavior therapy?" *Clinical Psychology Review* 27:2, 173-187. Online: http://www.sciencedirect.com/science/article/pii/S027273580600081X (retrieved 29 Jan. 2015). See also the discussion in my book *Of Two Minds*.

In the meantime, write to me, if you have a moment, and let me know what you think: kas.e.thomas@gmail.com. I'm interested to hear *your* story.

Kas Thomas
Jacksonville, Florida
9 February 2015

Depression Hacks

Save Some Compassion for Yourself

My wife, who suffers from depression (as I do; but hers is much worse), beats herself up a lot. She says horrible things about herself sometimes. "I'm a terrible person." "I have nothing interesting to say." "My thoughts don't matter." "I'm a failure at everything I do."

Do you have that little voice in your head sometimes, telling you what an idiot you are? How messed up you are? How disastrous your life is?

If you're constantly beating yourself up, take a step back; give yourself a break. You're suffering too much as it is.

Would you knowingly insult a stranger if you knew that person was suffering with some horrible illness? Would you bully a war vet who's in a wheelchair? No? Then why are you doing that to yourself?

Give yourself an I.O.U. today on self-punishment. Defer today's self-punishment. Replace it with compassion.

You've experienced traumas (big and small) in your life. Add them up sometime. Make a list of the traumas you've lived through. You might be surprised how long the list is. The traumas start in childhood, after all.

Have a talk with your inner child; the child-you that's still lurking inside you, somewhere. Console him or her. Acknowledge the hurt. Acknowledge the *legitimacy* of the hurt, the fact that it's *okay* to hurt; it's appropriate. This is not a pep-talk, so don't sugar-coat things. And don't judge. Just acknowledge that you're entitled to feel what you're feeling.

Getting other people to acknowledge your pain is not as important as reflecting on it *yourself*, first and foremost.

When you've recognized your pain, and its roots, in its awful totality, you will be able to console your inner child; and you'll both mourn. At that moment, you must put away self-recriminations and self-loathing.

The Root of All Evil

Poor Freud. We mock him so. Classical Freudian psychoanalytic theory, with its emphasis on Oedipal mother-love, father-hate, penis envy, infantile sexuality, etc., is essentially discredited now, to a large extent.

But Sigmund Freud was right about one thing. He knew, as Charcot and others knew before him, that almost all psychopathology, certainly the vast majority, stems ultimately from trauma. And it so happens that much of the trauma that causes problems in later life originates in childhood or adolescence. So to this extent, at least, we can say Freud was right—he was right to devote so much attention to people's early lives, and to the trauma people experience as children.

But trauma can occur at any point in life. And whenever it happens, it's a potential source of trouble for the mind.

The conscious mind is easily overloaded by harmful stimuli: death, pain, destruction, intimidation, violence, verbal abuse, intimidation, adversity, uncertainty, or the mere threat of these things. The logical parts of your mind can process only so many of these sorts of things without freezing up. The unprocessed excess has to go somewhere, so it goes to parts of your mind that can store, but not necessarily process, the information. Collectively, these parts of the mind are known to some experts (Freud, for instance) as the *unconscious mind*. Semi-processed information resides in the unconscious mind (perhaps forever), where it can stay dormant, or bubble up to the surface, from time to time, as dreams, hallucinations, delusions, fears, feelings of foreboding, deja-vu experiences, etc.

The scientific literature on psychopathology is vast and confusing (and much of it is of low quality), but the literature is extraordinarily clear on one thing, which is the relationship between trauma and mental illness.

The range of adult disorders in which childhood traumas have been shown to play an etiological role includes not only depression and PTSD but anxiety disorders, dissociative disorders, eating disorders, personality disorders, substance abuse, and sexual dysfunction, among others.[2]

With schizophrenia, the literature shows that the associations between childhood trauma and schizophrenia are actually as strong as *or stronger than* the associations between childhood trauma and less severe disorders.

A literature review by Read *et al.* (2005) found:

> Symptoms considered indicative of psychosis and schizophrenia, particularly hallucinations, are at least as strongly related to childhood abuse and neglect as many other mental health problems. Recent large-scale general population studies indicate the relationship is a causal one, with a dose-effect.[3]

The Read group concluded that "child abuse is a causal factor for psychosis and schizophrenia, and more specifically, for hallucinations, particularly voices commenting and command hallucinations," although Read also noted that "the study of the mechanisms linking child abuse and psychosis is still in its infancy and requires more research to evaluate, and integrate, the theories that have recently been proposed."

---

2 Beitchman, J. et al. (1992), "A review of the long-term effects of child sexual abuse," *Child Abuse and Neglect*, 16:101-18.

3 Read, J. *et al.* (2005), "Childhood trauma, psychosis and schizophrenia: a literature review with theoretical and clinical implications" *Acta Psychiatr Scand* 2005: 112: 330–350. Online at: http://www.psychrights.org/Articles/ACTAChildhoodTrauma2005.pdf (retrieved 27 Dec. 2014).

Think about what this means. Voices in your head (auditory hallucinations), visual hallucinations, delusions—psychotic symptoms, which occur not *just* in schizophrenia, but in severe depression, PTSD, and other disorders—can stem from trauma.

Every person's case is different. Your situation is unique to you. But if you're suffering from depression or other serious mental distress, odds are good you've suffered some kind of trauma.

Trauma is the root of all evil. It's where most mental illness starts. The literature is absolutely crystal clear on this.

The trauma can be from long ago or from something recent. It doesn't matter, because one thing we know about trauma is that the effects tend to linger. Even if you've been lucky enough to forget the memories surrounding your traumas, your nervous system never forgets. You can't unexperience a distressing event.

The effects of trauma thus accumulate over time (sometimes across generations; the phenomenon of intergenerational trauma is well studied). The effects add up. They contribute to what I call *trauma debt*, which is the unreconciled psychic distress you carry around, your whole life, due to accumulated trauma going back to childhood (or beyond, in the case of intergenerational trauma). Sometimes, the debt can be reduced. Sometimes it can be refinanced. Rarely is it forgiven.

Trauma debt can be postponed, but the bill always comes due. You pay for it in suffering. But you can "pay down" the debt, quite often, in therapy (with a little luck and a lot of hard work). The therapist's office is where you re-consolidate and refinance the debt in such a way that you can handle it, so that it's no longer crushing.

The bottom line is: *Don't underestimate the importance of trauma in your life.* Be clear on where your mental distress comes from: It almost certainly comes from past traumas. When you understand what your traumas are, and the effect(s) they've had on you, you're in a position to move forward.

Know Your Enemy

If you suffer from depression or any other kind of mental condition, you owe it to yourself to become educated on the condition. That doesn't mean reading *Psychology Today* articles or Wikipedia entries (although that's a start). It means digging deep, reading up on the *science*, becoming truly informed. Why is this so important? Because there's a lot of misinformation out there, and (sad to say) mental health care providers are not always up to date on the latest research. Or even the older research.

Ignorance is dangerous, especially when it comes to your health. You can't afford to buy into myths, half-truths, or someone's well-intentioned (but misinformed) feel-good philosophy that's based on little more than wishful thinking. You need to know *the facts*.

Doctors, nurse practitioners, licensed mental health counselors, and psychologists are only human. Some of them have unwittingly bought into a lot of the same myths you and I have been fed by the drug industry, NAMI, NIMH, APA, and others who have their own special agendas.

I believe in evidence-based medicine. (I'm not an anti-psychiatry crackpot. I do believe in looking *critically* at what goes on in the field, though.) I read a lot of scientific papers. You should too. It's not that hard. You should also seek out evidence-based books on mental illness. There are plenty of good ones out there.

For starters, you should consider reading Robert Whitaker's books *Mad in America* (2002, Basic Books) and *Anatomy of an Epidemic* (2010, Broadway Paperbacks). Whitaker is a former *Boston Globe* journalist. He has no ax to grind; he's just a great journalist and ace science writer. His books are filled with solid investigative reporting, backed up with tons of footnotes. They're easy to read , informative, and entertaining.

If you're taking antidepressants, you'll want to be sure to seek out Irving Kirsch's *The Emperor's New Drugs* (Random House and Basic Books, 2009 and 2010). Kirsch is a researcher and lecturer in medicine at the Harvard Medical School. His book is easy to read and filled with insights. It will give you much needed perspective on drugs for depression.

Also please consider my book *Of Two Minds* (Author-Zone Books, 2015)[4]. It's a much longer book than this one (400 physical pages, counting front and back matter), partly based on personal experience (in other words, part memoir) and part science reporting. It has over 300 footnotes, to give you direct pointers to the literature on depression, schizophrenia, antidepressants, talk therapy, studies about drugs, exercise, and so on. It's designed to be easy to read and entertaining. It busts myths and provides straight talk on therapeutic options.

I can't recap all the information you need to know in just a few pages. But I can give you a head start.

Probably one of the biggest myths about depression is the (mistaken) idea that it never goes away on its own. (Don't take this as advice to do nothing! I'm *not saying* to sit around and wait for it to go away on its own.) Depression is typically (though not always) *episodic* and often resolves on its own, without any professional or other interventions.[5] This fact is seldom discussed in books and articles on mental illness, yet it's fundamental to understanding the disorder.

---

4   ISBN-13: 978-1507753927 or ISBN-10: 1507753926.

5   The Royal College of Physicians (2010) says, on its web site: "The good news is that 4 out of 5 people with depression will get completely better without any help in about 4-6 months—sometimes more." See: http://www.rcpsych.ac.uk/mentalhealthinformation/mentalhealthproblems/depression/depression.aspx (retrieved 21 Jan. 2015).

18

Emil Kraepelin (1856–1926), who coined the term "manic depressive," found in his own research that in contrast to his patients suffering from *dementia praecox* (schizophrenia), those suffering manic depression had a relatively good prognosis, with 60% to 70% of patients suffering only one attack, and attacks lasting, on average, seven months.

Do we have modern, scientific evidence that people really get better on their own? We do, actually. In the Netherlands, in 2002, researchers looked at the progress of 250 patients who had presented with an episode of major depression. Two thirds of the patients were female, and for 43%, it was a repeat episode. Some patients sought treatment at the primary-care level; others sought mental-health-system care; others sought no care. The researchers found that the overwhelming majority of patients *eventually recovered* (defined as "no or minimal depressive symptoms in a 3-month period"), *regardless of the level of treatment.*[6]

Duration of major depressive episodes has been found to vary widely, with median durations between 3 months and 12 months and rates of chronicity (duration 24 months or more) between 10% and 30%.[7] In the Dutch study just mentioned, the median duration of major-depressive episodes was 3.0 months for those who had no professional care, 4.5 months for those who sought primary care, and 6.0 months for those who entered the mental health care system. The differences in episode duration could reflect severity. In other words,

6   Spijker *et al.* (2002), "Duration of major depressive episodes in the general population: results from The Netherlands Mental Health Survey and Incidence Study (NEMESIS)," *The British Journal of Psychiatry,* 181: 208-213 doi: 10.1192/bjp.181.3.208, available free online at: http://bjp.rcpsych.org/content/181/3/208.full, retrieved 7 Dec. 2014.

7   See Keller, M. B., *et al* (1982) "Recovery in major depression. Analysis with life tables and regression models." *Archives of General Psychiatry,* 39, 905 -910. Also see Furukawa, T. A., Kiturama, T. & Takahashi, K. (2000) "Time to recovery of an inception cohort with hitherto untreated unipolar major depressive episodes." *British Journal of Psychiatry,* 177, 331 -335. See also references cited in the Spijker paper mentioned previously.

the people who recovered quickly *on their own* may have done so because they were less depressed to begin with. It stands to reason that those who sought help at the mental-health-system level were probably *more* depressed, hence took longer to recover. Nevertheless, the Dutch study results show quite clearly that people who sought *no professional help* saw their depression get better in a shorter time frame (3 months) than people who sought care (4.5 to 6 months). That's not to say you should seek no care! I'm just telling you the facts. People do get better on their own, much of the time. So even if traditional sorts of interventions don't work for you, *that's not reason to give up all hope.*

The other thing you should know about depression is that it correlates with age. The older you are, the more likely depression is. Why should depression be more prevalent in older people? First, there's the obvious fact that the burden of disease is greater in older populations. We know that a diagnosis of serious somatic disease (diabetes, cardiovascular disease, obesity, cancer) is, for many, a trigger for depression. Also, the older you are, the more likely it is you'll experience loss: loss of a loved one (to death, disease, divorce, etc.), loss of a job, opportunity loss. Children grow up and leave home. Stuff happens. *Life* happens.

Whites (surprisingly enough) are more apt to complain of depression than other races. Women are more apt to self-report as depressed than men. In all likelihood, the gender gap here is not as great as one might think. Men are famously self-reliant and unlikely to ask for help. "If I get myself in trouble, I'll get myself out" is a prototypical male response to getting lost while driving. It's the same with depression, most likely. Women ask for help right away. Men don't.

Many studies have found an inverse correlation between income and depression. Data from the CDC (2011) show that if you are living below the poverty level ($11,490/yr., in the U.S., if you're single) and you're between the ages of 20 and 64, you're at roughly *five times greater risk of depression* than if you're making 400% or more of poverty level income ($45,960/yr, if you're single)[8].

The two most popular therapeutic options for depression are drugs and talk therapy. Depending on which studies you read, drugs are either extremely effective or barely more effective than placebo. The literature is skewed in favor of drug effectiveness, because (as Kirsch and others have demonstrated) many clinical trials that fail to show positive results simply don't get published, and most of the trials that do show strong results are underwritten by drug companies (and often use professional ghostwriters, with big-name doctors attached later as "guest authors"). The Sequenced Treatment Alternatives to Relieve Depression (STAR*D) study was easily the single largest study of its kind, ever, lasting six years and involving almost 4,000 patients in more than 40 treatment centers. It was a real-world study of patients in real-life clinical settings, not "controlled trials" settings. Over 100 scientific papers came out of that $35 million study. I talk about the STAR*D results in greater detail in *Of Two Minds*. But basically, the upshot of the study was that, using remission as an outcome standard, only 32.9% of patients in the initial phase of the study got better (taking Celexa). Patients who failed to get better in the first phase got to try a different drug in the second phase. In that phase, 30.6% of patients got better. In the third phase, 13.6% got better, and in the fourth and final phase 14.7% got better. These numbers are not additive. They represent raw success rates for independent phases of the trial. You should *average* them, not add them.

Almost exactly half of clinical trials submitted to FDA for approval of SSRIs (modern antidepressants) failed to show separation from placebo. In plain English, this means about half the time, studies designed to prove efficacy failed to prove efficacy. It doesn't mean no one got better in those trials. It means the number of people who got better on the drug was about the same as the number who got better on

---

8   http://www.cdc.gov/nchs/data/hus/hus11.pdf, retrieved 2 Dec 2014.

the placebo.

In trials that do show efficacy, results vary widely, but it's not uncommon to see 30% to 50% improvement (in averaged Hamilton depression-scale scores) for drug "responders" versus 20% to 30% improvement for placebo-takers.

Bottom line, the drugs work for some people, but can't be said (with a straight face) to be hugely effective for a majority of users.

Does this mean you shouldn't try the drugs? No, that's not what I'm saying at all. You *should* try anything that might work, even if the odds are 50-50 (or less). The drugs might work *for you.* You won't know until you try. So try them, but don't expect miracles.

The scientific literature on talk therapy is vast and confusing, but I think it's probably fair to say that talk therapy has been shown to be effective for many people (the percentage varies, according to which study you read; I hesitate to cite a number). It's effective so much of the time, it deserves to be considered a worthwhile option. To give you some of the flavor of the research, I'll cite one study in particular: The National Institute of Mental Health's Treatment of Depression Collaborative Research Project (TDCRP) compared Cognitive Behavioral Therapy (CBT), interpersonal therapy (IPT), antidepressant therapy (imipramine[9]), and placebo, in a carefully designed trial. Followup assessments were conducted at 6, 12, and 18 months after treatment. Of all patients entering treatment and having followup data, the proportion who recovered (eight weeks of minimal or no symptoms following the end of treatment) did not differ remarkably among the four treatments: 36% for those in the CBT group, 43% for those in the interpersonal therapy (IPT) group, 42% for those in the imipramine plus clinical management (CM) group, and 21% for those in the placebo plus CM group. Among patients who recovered, relapse rates were 36% for CBT, 33% for IPT, 50% for imipramine plus CM, and 33% for those in the placebo plus CM group.[10] The best predictor

---

9 Tofranil (a tricyclic antidepressant).
10 Elkin, I. *et al.* (1989), "National Institute of Mental Health treatment of

of outcome across all four groups was the quality of the relationship between patient and therapist (as perceived by the patient) early in treatment. (Note that patients who did not take medication had lower rates of relapse. Also note, 32% of patients dropped out of the study early; 9% got worse, suffering an iatrogenic outcome.[11])

The study I just cited used a fairly strict outcome measure: remission. Most studies simply look for improvement. In those that look just for *improvement*, response percentages tend to be higher, of course.

In medicine (and psychology), there are a lot of what I like to call "31% solutions"—things that tend to work about 31% of the time.

Antidepressants tend to work about 31% of the time.

Placebos work about 31% of the time.

Talk therapy arguably works more than 31% of the time.

Low-dose shock therapy works about 31% of the time (but so does sham ECT). Shock therapy is damaging to the memory, however, which means it probably works by making you forget about your troubles. (Read the Appendix in this book about Electroconvulsive Therapy for details.)

Alcoholics Anonymous seems to work about 31% of the time. (That's the year-over-year continuation rate for people who join.)

Physical exercise tends to work about 31% of the time.

People who seek no treatment at all tend to improve about 31% of the time.

No one's done the study, but I imagine talking to your dog tends to work about 31% of the time.

All of these things work for some people, some of the time. But because every person's situation is unique, they all work for different people. And you won't know what works *for you* until you try it.

---

depression collaborative research program: general effectiveness of treatments," *Archives of General Psychiatry,* Vol. 46, 971-82. Online: http://www.safranlab.net/uploads/7/6/4/6/7646935/nimh_1.pdf (retrieved 15 Jan. 2015).

11 An iatrogenic outcome means the patient got worse instead of better.

So do your research, and try the therapeutic options that seem best suited to your sensibilities. If one modality doesn't work, try another one. Eventually, you'll find something that works.

Don't simply buy into the myths that drugs work all the time, that antidepressants fix a "chemical imbalance in the brain" (there's no credible scientific evidence for that theory), that CBT is more effective than other modalities (it might be, for some people, but overall it's not), that shock therapy is guaranteed to work (it definitely is not), etc. The myths will lead you astray and leave you bitter. Don't buy into them. Do your own homework. Do what works *for you*.

Why You Cling to Feel-Bad Strategies

It's trendy now to say "happiness is a choice," but in fact, as every depression sufferer knows, things are not quite that simple. If happiness *were* a choice, everyone would choose it. The end.

Unhappiness is not a choice any of us wants to make, but we somehow end up less happy than we intend, often through coping mechanisms (and self-medication techniques involving junk food, tobacco, or alcohol) that are less than optimal, to put it mildly.

Still, poor coping mechanisms—choices that ultimately undermine our subjective sense of well-being—are incredibly popular. I've often wondered why this is so, even though I myself have used poor coping mechanisms in the past: avoidance, social withdrawal, denial, catastrophizing, alcohol abuse, passive-aggressive behavior—you name it, I've probably tried it.

The problem with using *unhappiness* strategies is that they become habits that are hard to break. We just get more miserable. And yet, such strategies must have *some* usefulness, or we wouldn't cling to them.

It's not that people *want* to feel bad. But feel-bad strategies do have a certain appeal.

If I feel bad, I won't have to feel as guilty.
If I feel bad, it proves I'm a decent person.
If I feel bad, I am assuming responsibility.
If I feel bad, I am not hurting anybody.
If I feel bad, it means I'm working on something.
If I feel bad, it proves I'm realistic.
If I feel bad, it proves I'm sensitive.

And so on.

Feel-bad strategies represent a "comfort zone" of their own, a place that may not be completely satisfying, but is at least *familiar* (and thus not scary).

The appeal of familiarity and predictability can be formidable. We *crave* familiarity. We crave anything that keeps terror out.

Let me ask you something. Have you ever wondered why McDonalds is the most successful restaurant chain in the world? Think about it for a moment. No one (that I know of) accuses McDonalds of having fantastic food. No McDonalds location carries a three-star Michelin Guide rating. Many people consider the food quite mediocre, even abysmal. How in the world, then, does McDonalds continue to enjoy such huge success? *What's the secret?*

The secret, in a nutshell, is familiarity; predictability. Consistency.

When you go to a McDonalds outlet, anywhere in the world, you *know,* in advance, what the experience is going to be like. You know, down to the last detail, what the food will be like, what the décor is going to be like, what the prices are, what kind of service to expect, and so on. No surprises.

Modern life is so random and perverse, so filled with confusing *choices* (demanding that we constantly make decisions), so laden with unexpected exigencies, many of them frightening, that people *crave* the sheer monotony of the McDonalds experience, the *guarantee* that absolutely nothing challenging, scary, or out of the ordinary will occur while eating at McDonalds.

Take stock, sometime, of your coping mechanisms. Be honest about how good, or how lousy, they are. But notice one thing. You cling to them because of *familiarity,* like a pair of old shoes that are fugly and smelly but comfortable (so you wear them anyway).

Your coping strategies, if they include things like social withdrawal, denial, overgeneralizing, magnifying negatives, minimizing positives, passive-aggressive behaviors, losing your temper, self-medicating with things that are bad for you, etc., probably aren't working all that well for you. They're kinda/sorta doing the job, but leaving you unhappy in the end. You cling to them out of habit, because of familiarity. Your feel-bad strategies aren't totally working, *yet you keep on using them.* Which means, at the level of coping strategies, you're eating at McDonalds.

Know one thing: Eating at McDonalds is a choice. Nobody is *forced* to eat there. You eat there because you choose to do so.

Decide where you want to eat—literally, and figuratively.

Give Yourself an I.O.U.

This is an important tip. Bear in mind, though, it's just *one tip*, not a cure for everything. It's *one* tool, of many, you should keep in your grab-bag of tools for maintaining mental health.

The tip is this: If you are having a compulsion to take a drug (e.g., alcohol), eat a food you shouldn't eat, or engage in a habit you're trying to break yourself of, immediately give yourself an I.O.U. Tell yourself: I will *allow* myself this indulgence (this drink, this piece of cake, this unnecessary purchase, this whatever-it-happens-to-be), later, but *not right this minute*. For example, say you're on a diet, but you desperately want a piece of cake that's staring you in the face. Tell yourself you'll eat it, but *not now*. Put it away and defer the enjoyment of it for later. If a nagging, child-like inner voice keeps saying *"But I want it now!"* you have to be the adult in this situation and *tell* your inner child, politely but firmly, that the decision has already been made: You can have it, *later.*

Any time an inner voice tells you the wrong thing, you have to stop and ask yourself, honestly: Is that really the *adult* you, or is it the *child* you? We all have an inner child; and it's important to nurture it. But as an adult, it's your responsibility not to let a petulant child rule you. Sometimes you really do have to have that talk with your inner child. Just say: "Okay, I hear you. All right? You've been heard. Now let's get on with things."

Studies have shown that if you give yourself permission to indulge in a harmful behavior *later*, you're less likely to do the harmful behavior now *or* later. If you can successfully defer the activity, you increase your odds of not doing it at all.

Giving yourself *permission* to do something is an important key to defusing the irresistible attraction of "naughty" behaviors. The forbiddenness of a forbidden activity is part of what makes the activity compelling. When it's no longer forbidden, it loses some of the excitement. Any parent knows this. If you put a child in a room with a book and say "Whatever you do, *don't open this book*," then you leave the room, odds are the child will open the book as soon as you're gone. But if you repeat the experiment without saying "Don't open the book," the child probably won't open the book.

If you give yourself permission to eat dessert later, you may eat the dessert later, or you may find that by the time you've had some real food, or engaged in some exercise, showered, talked on the phone with someone, or whatever, you're no longer in a frenzy to eat the dessert. Maybe you eat the half the dessert. Or maybe you eat all of it, 75% of the time—which is still an improvement of 25% over the usual trick of *denying* yourself a dessert, then impulsively eating it *because* it's forbidden.

This same trick can be used for alcohol ("I'll have that extra drink later, instead of now"), impulse purchases ("I'll treat myself later, just not this minute"), and many other kinds of temptations. *Defuse the temptation* by giving yourself permission. Deal with the temptation later. You'll find that a good percentage of the time, later never comes.

Balance Is Important

In the past, when my mood has gone haywire, I've noticed that, quite often, things in my life were out of balance—skewed in some way. My sleep habits might have been all over the map. My eating habits might have taken a left turn (into carbohydrates, away from protein; or into binge eating—junk food). My daily routine, quite often, was no longer a routine, but an ad hoc Hodge-podge of mayhem.

Shouldn't you strive for some kind of *balance* in your life?

Temporal balance (time allocation) is a big problem. Many times, I've found myself spending the majority of my thoughts on future problems; or (alternatively) worrying about things that happened in the past—*no balance at all* between past, present, and future. My father used to annoy me, at times, by saying: "Don't forget to stop and smell the roses!" What he was trying to say is: Don't spend so much time thinking about yesterday, or tomorrow, that you fail to *seize the day*. It's easy (too easy) to get wrapped up in worrying about things that haven't happened yet—or things that *did* happen, that you have no control over. But ask yourself: Should you allow your mind get so weathervaned by these other concerns that you let yourself be *overwhelmed* by them, to the point of not noticing what's going on right now, in front of you? Shouldn't you spend at least *half* your waking thoughts thinking about the here and now? *All we have*, really, is the here and now. Past and future are figments of the imagination. Why are you spending so much time on them?

Look at your eating habits, your sleep habits, your thought habits, your work habits, your spending habits. Ask yourself, objectively, whether there's a glaring imbalance somewhere. Take at least *some* steps to try to mitigate the imbalance. It doesn't have to mean taking drastic action (although it could). It just means: start by being *mindful* of the imbalances. Be conscious of them. Don't let them get to the point where they *rule* you. Introduce balance where you can. Start small, but get the needle moving in the right direction.

Use the I.O.U. Method: Set a time limit on a problem activity, and when the time is up, promise yourself *you'll return to it later.* Odds are, when you return to it, you won't be so fixated on it; you'll bring a more objective frame of mind; you'll be more apt to bring clarity and mindfulness to the activity.

Balance is important. Attend to it.

Control Your Mind's "Raw Data"

Your mind is like a computer, processing raw inputs (sensory inputs, as well as thoughts and memories) all day. If you feed your mind low-quality input, isn't it bound to result in low-quality output? If 90% of what comes into your mind through your eyes and ears is negative or frightening or contradictory, isn't that eventually going to affect how you think? As they say in the computer business: *Garbage in, garbage out.*

Let me tell you a secret. You are almost certainly underestimating the amount of low-quality, potentially harmful negative garbage that enters your mind (through your senses) every day. One of the chief sources of such negativity is *news*: news from TV, particularly, but also from the Internet (Buzzfeed, HuffPost, etc.), magazines, newspapers, and other media sources.

Steve Chandler, in *100 Ways to Motivate Yourself* (Career Press, 2004), talks about the time he worked for a city newspaper. "I remember how hard the editors in the newsroom would search for the most shocking stories they could find," he recalls. "I saw how panicked the city desk got if there were no murders or rapes that day. I watched as they tore through the wire stories to see if a news item from another state could be gruesome enough to save the front page. If there's no drowning, they'll reluctantly go with a near-drowning."

The news is designed to horrify. Steve Chandler explains: "The news is not the news. It is the *bad news*. It is deliberate shock. The more you accept it as the news, the more you believe that 'that's the way it is,' and the more fearful and cynical you will become."

News editors deliberately pick high-shock-value stories, not just to sell more newspapers or juice the online traffic stats but to give advertisers more bang for their buck. TV stations understand very well that if you can heighten the emotions of viewers, just before going to a station break, people bring those heightened emotions to the viewing of advertisements; as a result, they're more likely to call the 800 number, go to the Geico website, ask their doctor if Abilify is right for them, or take whatever action an advertiser wants to provoke. *Viewers who are in a heightened state of emotional arousal react more viscerally to TV ads.* This is well known by CNN, Fox News, and the rest, who routinely bookend station breaks with shock-and-awe news stories.

To avoid being manipulated in this fashion, you should consider going on a news fast. Try cutting TV and internet news out of your day once in a while. Start with one day a week. Expand it to multiple days a week. Try the "news fast" experiment, and see what happens to your state of mind. You may find that the world becomes a more convivial place after you cut back on the unending stream of toxic doom-and-gloom porn served up by news outlets.

Emerson said "We become what we think about all day long." If you leave what you think about to chance, or to whatever's on TV (or radio, etc.), you're losing a large measure of control over your own mind. *Exercise conscious control over what enters your brain.* Don't leave it to chance. If you do, your brain will fill up with toxic nonsense in a hurry.

Avoid Negative People

In addition to going on a "news fast," you should consider going on a people fast in which you route around cynics, doubters, complainers, doom-and-gloomers, and others who bring negativity into your life. This can be a hard rule to put into practice, if you live with someone who's negative. It could mean filing for divorce. If you're working around negative people, you may need to look for another job. If your best friend is negative, it may mean finding a new best friend.

When you get into a conversation with a cynic, hope has a way of dissolving. Your sense of possibilities dwindles. Fatalism and pessimism become the new normal. That's not what you want. Is it?

I have a friend, whom I've known for many years, who's dismissive of new ideas and has an extraordinarily cynical view of human nature ("people are stupid" is one of his hallmark beliefs). He's inherently contentious and pooh-poohs a new ideas without even considering where the idea came from or why it exists in the first place. Like a lot of negative people, he flatters himself that he's a critical thinker, as if cynicism is the mark of a discriminating intelligence. A critical thinker, though, is someone who can knowledgeably and dispassionately assess the relative merits of an idea based on its assumptions and the quality of existing evidence. That's not the same as simply criticizing everything, all the time. A *criticizer* is not the same as a critical thinker. It's funny how many people fail to see the distinction.

I've learned to block out my friend's kneejerk negativity. I value his friendship too much to simply blow him off. (We go way back.) But I do sometimes have to "turn the volume down" on his cantankerous, contrary, often nonsensical worldview.

Maybe you have friends like that, too. If so, learn how to "turn the volume down." Introduce a little distance. That doesn't mean you need to cut off all contact entirely (although it *could* mean that, if the other person is truly toxic.) When the other person says something negative, say something positive. It's unlikely you'll change that person's worldview (which, after all, took years to develop). But you can push back on the negativity now and then. Don't just nod your head and take it.

Andrew Weil, in *Spontaneous Healing*, says: "Make a list of friends and acquaintances in whose company you feel more alive, happier, more optimistic. Pick one whom you will spend some time with this week."

Enthusiasm is contagious. So is negativity. Choose between them.

Tapping, EFT, and EMDR

A variety of forms of evidence, including studies of populations exposed to natural disasters as well as research involving childhood trauma victims (and other types of studies as well), point to the fact that PTSD (post-traumatic stress disorder) and depression are linked. Preexisting depression tends to increase one's risk for PTSD[12], and a diagnosis of PTSD tends to predispose one to a later diagnosis of depression.[13] Work by Breslau *et al.* (2001) has tended to rule out the idea that PTSD and major depression stem from separate vulnerabilities in trauma-exposed victims.[14] They seem to come from the same place, even though not everyone who gets one gets the other —because adaptation to trauma is highly individual. It's tempting to speculate that PTSD and depression are basically two different forms of the same thing, on different parts of a spectrum. Maybe depression, in this view, is a kind of retrograde PTSD.

Because PTSD and depression are related, you might want to be aware of how treatment for PTSD works, since depression is often due to trauma and may respond to the same sorts of strategies people use

---

12 Bromet E., Sonnega A., Kessler R.C. (1998), "Risk factors for DSM-III-R posttraumatic stress disorder: Findings from the National Comorbidity Survey," *Am J Epidemiol* 147:353–361.

13 Kessler R.C., Sonnega A., Bromet E., Nelson C.B. (1995), "Posttraumatic stress disorder in the National Comorbidity Survey," *Arch Gen Psychiatry* 52:1048–1060.

14 Breslau *et al.* (2001), "A second look at comorbidity in victims of trauma: the posttraumatic stress disorder–major depression connection," *Biological Psychiatry* 48:9, 902-909, online at:
http://www.biologicalpsychiatryjournal.com/article/S0006-3223(00)00933-1/pdf (retrieved 26 Dec. 2014).

in dealing with PTSD.

Various techniques have been tried for PTSD. Three that are worth looking into are the rewind method, eye movement desensitization and reprocessing (EMDR), and emotional freedom techniques (EFT). Not all clinicians think highly of these techniques (a kind way of saying, you'll encounter a lot of prejudice against these techniques among certain therapists who've done a tiny bit of homework and decided these methods are a lot of hocus-pocus without theoretical basis). My recommendation is that you do your own reading on these matters and decide for yourself. These techniques have helped a lot of people, on that basis alone they're worth looking into. But also, there are good, sound theoretical reasons to believe these techniques can work (see discussion further below); and the evidence base, while not yet strong, is growing rapidly.

The rewind technique is a visualization technique that begins when the patient is in a calm, relaxed state. The patient images that in his or her special place of safety, he/she has a television set and a video player with a remote control device. The patient is asked to imagine floating to one side, out of body, where he can watch himself watching the TV screen. The patient imagines *watching himself watch* a "film" of the traumatic event that led to the PTSD. The film begins at a point before the trauma occurred and ends at a point at which the trauma is over, when it's safe again. The patient's job is to float back into his body and experience watching the trauma in reverse, as if the TV has been commanded to "rewind the tape." Then the patient "watches" the "video" as if pressing the fast-forward button. This "watching" of the "video" of the memory, in fast-reverse and fast-forward modes, is repeated at whatever speed feels comfortable, and as many times as needed, until the scenes evoke no emotion from the patient.

It's an interesting technique, isn't it? Three levels of voyeurism. The patient imagines (level one) a scene in which the patient, removed from his own body, is watching himself (level two) on a couch in front of a TV, watching a video (level three) of a traumatic past event. The voyeuristic detachment provides extra degrees of safety and control; then the control aspect is fortified by having the patient's *imagined self* exercise control of the TV image through a remote control. The trauma, meanwhile, plays out not as an accurate 3D memory, but as a flat image *on a TV screen*. (It might help even more to imagine that the TV image is black and white, or grainy.) The fact that the patient controls the image through a remote control reinforces the (healing) notion that you're in control of your mind. But also, the fact that the patient can play the trauma-video backwards, at any point and at any speed, reinforces the belief that trauma may be reversible.

If you ask me, it's a brilliant technique, and I'm not surprised to learn that it works for many people. We'll talk about *why* it works in a minute.

Eye movement desensitization and reprocessing (EMDR) was "discovered" in 1987 by Francine Shapiro, at the time a clinical psychology student in California, who refined it into a highly specific treatment for which, originally, there were numerous supporters, including many eminent professors of psychology. It was recently recommended as a treatment for PTSD by the National Institute for Clinical Excellence (NICE) in the UK.

Over time, the literature on EMDR has become mixed, with some researchers claiming its effectiveness is no greater than with placebo. Others have found that the eye movements do not inhibit negative emotions and that the reprocessing element doesn't play a significant role in any positive outcome. There is no question, however, that EMDR has helped people, and in a recent study it was found to be as effective as, or perhaps even slightly more effective than, EFT (also known as "tapping," which I'll talk about in a minute).

EMDR is grounded in the adaptive information processing model, which says that pathology is a consequence of incorrectly or in-completely processed distressing past experiences. It has a multi-phase protocol that addresses past, present, and future contributors to distress. The treatment includes:

1. History-taking. What was the original traumatizing event? Identify problem memories, triggers, etc.

2. Preparation. The therapist helps the client develop ways to cope with distressing emotions so that he/she is able to calm down and cope better between therapy sessions. Commonly this is done with guided imagery or other relaxation techniques

3. Assessment. The client will be asked to describe a thought or negative cognition (NC) associated with an image that encapsulates the traumatizing event. The client is also asked to develop a *positive cognition* (PC) to be associated with the same image that is desired in place of the negative one The desired positive belief is rated on a Validity of Cognition Scale and the emotion felt is rated on a Subjective Unit of Discomfort Scale.

4. Desensitization. During the reprocessing phases of EMDR therapy, the patient focuses on the disturbing memory in multiple brief sets of about 15–30 seconds. Simultaneously, the patient will focus on the dual attention stimulus, which consists of focusing on the trauma while the clinician initiates lateral eye movement, or another stimulus such as a pulsing light held in each hand, or tapping on the knees. Following each set, the patient is asked what associative information was elicited during the procedure. This new material usually becomes the focus of the next set, or another aspect of the memory may be guided by the clinician. This process of personal association is repeated many times during the session and continues until the patient no longer feels as distressed when thinking of the target memory.

5. Installation. The therapist asks the patient to focus on the event along with the positive cognition developed in step 3. The patient is asked to hold in mind the positive thought as the therapist continues with the bilateral stimulation. When the patient feels he or she is certain the positive cognition is assimilated, to the maximum degree possible, the installation phase is complete.

6. Body scan. In this phase, the goal of the therapist is to identify any uncomfortable sensations that are lingering in the body when the

patient is thinking about the target memory and the positive cognition (PC). The patient (while thinking about the PC) is asked to scan over his or her body entirely, searching for tension, tightness, or other physical sensation. Any negative sensations are targeted, then diminished, using the same bilateral stimulation technique from phases 4 and 5.

7. Closure. The therapist will teach the client relaxation techniques designed to bring about emotional stability and tranquility.

8. Reevaluation. At every new session, the therapist and patient will reevaluate the work done in the prior session and use that information to guide future work.

EMDR has had a controversial history, but there is no doubt that it has, in fact, worked for many people. A fairly recent, well designed study comparing EMDR with EFT found large effect sizes (of $d = 1.1$ for EMDR and 1.0 for EFT), with improvement happening more rapidly in the EMDR group than the EFT group.[15]

Why does EMDR work? We'll get to that in a second. But first, let's take a look at "tapping."

The so-called tapping technique springs initially from the work of American clinical psychologist Roger J. Callahan, who developed what he called "thought field therapy." The latter involved tapping (with fingertips) meridian points on the body (similar to acupuncture points), while recalling a traumatic event and (re)experiencing the extreme discomfort associated with the event. In Callahan's technique, particular meridian points release and re-balance energies preferentially for different types of trauma.

The emotional freedom technique (EFT) is a simplified version of thought field therapy, developed by Gary Craig, who trained with Callahan. It involves tapping the meridian points in turn, while

---

15 Karakzias et al. (2011), "A Controlled Comparison of the Effectiveness and Efficiency of Two Psychological Therapies for Posttraumatic Stress Disorder Eye Movement Desensitization and Reprocessing vs. Emotional Freedom Techniques," J Nerv Ment Dis 199, 372-378, online at http://painmuse.org/wp-content/uploads/emotionalfreedom_ptsd.pdf (retrieved 3 Feb. 2015).

recalling a stressful event, experiencing it, identifying the nature of the feelings that come up, verbalizing them, and accepting or reframing them. For detailed description of the technique and how to do it yourself, go to http://eft.mercola.com/.

As with EMDR, EFT has its detractors. Some of their complaints about literature bias are probably valid, but most scientific literature on psychiatric drugs and treatments are subject to the same complaints. What you should care about is whether people have actually been helped—which they have been. What you should also care about is whether there's any theoretical basis for believing these techniques should work at all. And there is.

First, you should know about something called the *orientation response*. The orientation response is the name given to the electrical signal in the brain that alerts us to any surprising or unexpected stimulus that interrupts normal routine. (Pavlov called it the curiosity reflex.) Research with animals as well as humans has shown that the most reliable stimulus for triggering the orientation response is movement. It grabs our attention at once. This is why TV commercials, for example, rely so much on sudden movement—because the eyes keep tracking it and we keep paying attention. It's also why, if you're explaining something to someone (in a meeting, perhaps, or in a classroom setting) and a visual distraction involving movement happens, you're apt to go into a state of temporary amnesia and forget what you were talking about. The orientation response causes us to suspend our normal processing so we can see if the sudden stimulus is potentially harmful or not.

Of course, if we were to lose track of what we were doing every time the orientation response is triggered, it would clearly be counter-productive and pose a risk, not an aid, to survival. If we're reading a book or cooking a meal when we're unexpectedly distracted, we have associative links—the book, the food—to draw us back to reality; back to where we were. But when we are talking or thinking, there is nothing to orient ourselves by. This is why so often, we might decide on an action, such as retrieving a needed item from the basement (or a closet, or bedroom, or whatever), but become engrossed in another thought en route—and find ourselves unable to remember what we had intended to fetch.

When visual stimulation is given in EMDR or you notice the movement created by tapping meridian points in EFT, and when the expectation is created that these meridian points are going to produce a powerful benefit, the therapist is actually setting up a powerful curiosity and expectation, and a whole series of orientation responses are fired off. This makes the brain susceptible to the same mild amnesia that makes you forget why you went to the basement to look for something.

The orientation response often happens when we are dreaming (have you noticed how many dreams involve movement?), to help facilitate the forgetting of emotional expectations from the previous day. Quite often, when were dreaming, different parts of our brain are doing different things, sometimes in coordination with each other but sometimes not. The amygdala, which is the primitive "fight or flight" organ of the brain, the part of the brain that stimulates fear or avoidance, becomes active on its own. The hippocampus, which is the part of your brain that prioritizes, categorizes, contextualizes, and "files away" memories, needs to be involved in processing memories in order for them to be stored correctly. But in a scary dream, the hippocampus is bypassed and you wake up thinking you're being attacked, or the house is on fire, or you're running away from something; and then you open your eyes and your neocortex (the "intelligent" part of your brain) tells you you're not really being attacked, the house isn't on fire, etc., and suddenly you can "sort out" what's going on.

In PTSD, the amygdala goes wild (with fright) and sensory inputs flood your brains with horrific images, bypassing the stunned hippocampus. Thus the images get stored inappropriately. There's an old saying in neuroscience: *neurons that fire together wire together.* If you see a school bus get smashed by a freight train at a railroad crossing, while the railroad-crossing warning bell is clanging, your overloaded brain may process the experience in such a way that from that day forward, any time you hear the clang-clang-clang of a bell you also see (or "feel") the disaster of a bus hit by a train. You associate bells with danger or fear.

In therapy, you need to disentangle those stimuli and reprocess them in a way that's no longer scary. A possible way to do that is to engage the neocortex in a distraction (watching yourself watch a video; tapping; bilateral eye movement) while the amygdala is in a *calm* state, so that the hippocampus can take time to process the information in an orderly way. If you can harness the orientation response to induce mild amnesia, long enough for the hippocampus to reprocess the data (without interference from an over-excited amygdala), the net result should be a reintegrated memory. And this is, indeed, what seems to happen in these therapeutic modalities: rewind technique, EFT, EMDR. When the techniques are successful, it's like waking up from a dream: you realize you're not really in danger, the events are understandable, a context is available for understanding what went on.

The studies for EFT and EMDR are often criticized for being of short duration (four sessions, for example); but this ignores the critical fact—and it is a fact, amazingly—that there are documented cases on record of people with PTSD having been *cured* of their PTSD in as little as one treatment session.

So before you pooh-pooh things like tapping and EMDR (or the rewind method), stop and consider that these techniques *have* actually helped people with very serious problems, and they do have a plausible theoretical basis.

But don't just take my word for it. Do a little research on your own, then seek out a therapist with appropriate training and a long history of treating PTSD. You may actually be able to obtain relief from your traumas using these techniques.

Reject False Schemas

A good first step in claiming control over your life and moods is to reject victim status. But this is harder to do than it seems.

Hear me out for a second.

Aaron T. Beck's cognitive theory of depression says that depressed people think the way they do because their thought processes are biased toward unreasonably negative interpretations[16]. According to this theory, depressed people acquire a *negative schema* of the world in childhood, as an effect of stressful life events, and the negative schema is activated later in life when the person encounters stressful situations.

Beck observed that depressed patients often present three types of negative beliefs (something he called the *cognitive triad*), which include negative thoughts about:

- the self (i.e., the self is worthless)
- the world/environment (i.e., the world is unfair), and
- the future (i.e., the future is hopeless).

The goal of psychotherapy, in Beck's view, is to reprogram the individual in such a way as to identify, then mitigate or eliminate, "bad coping skills" like arbitrary inference, selective abstraction, over-generalization, magnification, and minimization.

That's all well and good, but what you also have to realize is that all

---

16 Beck, Aaron T.; Rush, A. John; Shaw, Brian F.; Emery, Gary. (1979). *Cognitive Therapy of Depression.* New York: The Guilford Press. pp. 11. ISBN 0-89862-919-5

of us, whether we're aware of it or not, obtain certain schemata not just from our parents, siblings, and peers, but from the society in which we grow up. American society, in particular, fosters certain myths that become part of your nervous system. The myth of the self-made millionaire is one such distortion. If you've heard of (and accepted, without questioning) the term "self-made millionaire," you've been infected. Anyone who gives careful thought to that term will realize that it is deceptive: No one person can possibly do everything that goes into making himself or herself a millionaire. People like Ray Kroc (creator of the McDonalds franchise), Walt Disney, and Bill Gates built their fortunes with the help of *thousands* of hard-working ordinary people whose labors fed into these business pioneers' "success." In what sense is Bill Gates *self-made*, if he relied on tens of thousands of Microsoft employees (and millions of computer customers) to build his fortune? The entire concept of the self-made man is a ridiculous distortion.

America also teaches the dogma that we live in a land of opportunity, where hard work pays off and anyone can succeed. Ironically, the evidence offered in favor of this distorted worldview often takes the form of one-off success stories of the Bill Gates or Walt Disney kind—statistical outliers. The clear implication is that if you can't become a millionaire, *it's your own fault.* You didn't work hard enough;. You're not worthy. There's something wrong with *you.*

The self-reliance culture always puts the blame on the *individual.*

Look around the Internet and you'll see headlines like "Are You Making These 10 Mistakes of Marketing [or Health, or Career Growth, or your sex life, or whatever]?" The implication is that if your business or website or love life or career isn't doing well, it's because *you're making mistakes.* Whatever's keeping you down is *your fault.*

The Law of Attraction is another blame-the-victim scheme (or *schema*). If success hasn't found you, it's because you aren't doing the right things to *attract* it! Exactly how the Law of Attraction is a *law* (like the law of gravity) isn't explained.

Your Twitter timeline is full of these sorts of distorted messages. Marketers are forever peddling false-hope headlines that imply "you're not doing it right." LinkedIn is full of articles telling you why you're not getting that job, not getting that promotion, not getting the callback, not making the big bucks, not going further in your career, not getting more traffic to your blog.

An especially popular theme, at the moment, is the "This successful person began with failure" theme. Articles talk about the mistakes Jeff Bezos made in Amazon's early days, the investing mistakes made by Warren Buffett, etc. The underlying message: Even someone who *fails* can be a huge success, so *what's your excuse?*

Another popular theme is: *This famous person* (Steve Jobs, for example) *didn't finish college, yet ended up a billionaire.* The underlying message: You went to college and aren't a billionaire, hence you must be an incredible loser. (Or maybe you *didn't* go to college, and you're not a billionaire. You're still a loser!)

Look at the cover of *Cosmopolitan* magazine. Are you not pleasing your man in bed? It's obviously because *you didn't follow these five simple tips!* Are you not able to *find* a man? It's because you're not dressing a certain way, acting a certain way, using a certain dating site, wearing a certain perfume, reading a certain article.

It's impossible to live in today's culture and not be bombarded with this sort of nonsense. As a result, it's *inevitable* that you will incorporate self-blame into your psychology, your way of comprehending reality, your *schema*. It's a non-negotiable requirement of buying into the American Dream that you take full responsibility for your success (or lack of it). And therefore, as long as you're on a success track, as long as you can weave a satisfying narrative for your life (because you have job, have an upward career trajectory, have a spouse, have kids, have a house and car, have a 401K), you will coexist amicably with the cultural narratives in which you've been brought up. But when you stumble—when you lose your job and can't find another one (or you do, but the new job doesn't pay what the old one did), when you get divorced (or can't find a mate to begin with), when you buy a house that goes down in value, when you reach retirement age without a million dollars in your 401K, when you get cancer (because you didn't eat right, take the right supplements, read the right articles; remember, it's *your* fault you have cancer)—that's when you begin to blame yourself (and/or society, and/or your circumstances) for your problems, and *that's* when, all of a sudden, the Aaron T. Becks of the world decide you have the wrong *schema*. Because once again, it's your fault! *You've got the wrong schema!*

In point of fact, you were handed your schema by society long ago. You didn't have any say in the matter. You were raised in a society that promulgates distorted beliefs designed to offer hope (ostensibly) while in fact putting the blame for your problems squarely on *you*.

Since you've been raised in this kind of milieu your entire life, it will take you a long time to counter these negative beliefs. The first step is to realize they exist. These messages *do* exist; they're everywhere. Once you're aware of them, you'll be amazed to see how far-reaching they are.

Director John Carpenter, in 1988, made a science fiction movie called *They Live*. It's a wonderful low-budget thriller. In it, the main character finds that with the aid of special sunglasses, he can see that society has been infiltrated (and largely taken over) by aliens. When he puts the special glasses on and looks at a billboard, it says, in huge block letters, CONSUME. The cover of a magazine says OBEY. Hidden messages, visible only with the glasses on, say SUBMIT, BUY, DO NOT QUESTION AUTHORITY.

Your value system, your schema, comes partly from your parents and peers, but it also comes partly from the social milieu in which you find yourself, which is full of hidden messages. The messages say some pretty awful things: If you are not a success, it's your fault. If you're in pain, you're not normal. If you're depressed, it's because you didn't choose happiness. ("Happiness is a choice" is one of the many corrosive half-truths propagated by pop culture, to keep you a compliant consumer.)

Be aware of the manipulative subliminal messages contained in almost every article and advertisement you see online or on TV. Be *aware* of them and *reject* them. They're designed to keep you down, keep you compliant, passive; keep you blaming yourself.

Fight back.

If you've traveled outside the U.S., you no doubt have noticed that in other countries, gasoline is much more expensive. Food often is, as well (although alcohol generally isn't). I was in Basel, Switzerland a couple years ago. A "Whopper Meal" at Burger King was thirteen Swiss francs—about $17 U.S., at the time.

In the United States., we're blessed (or cursed, depending) with absurdly low gasoline prices, low food prices, affordable broadband, affordable cable TV. These are all narcotics that keep us mollified and submissive; we sleep through major elections, barely participating in our "participatory democracy," meanwhile cursing the venality of our Congressional (and other) leaders while doing nothing about it. In Roman times, the emperors knew very well that the answer to keeping the populace from revolting was "bread and circuses"—abundant food, low-cost entertainment; diversions. In the absence of diversions, people become more demanding. They start to demand things to which they are rightfully entitled—not phony promises of "opportunity" but *real* things, like employment, health care, education. The U.S. is one of few civilized countries on earth that doesn't provide guaranteed health care for its citizens (except the most expensive-to-insure citizens: older people and the disabled, who are covered by Medicare). For all the grandiose talk of American being "the greatest country on earth," we have no full-employment policy and *millions* of people who want to work are out of work. We have "the greatest education system on earth" but it costs almost $50,000 a year to go to a good college. In Libya (and Germany, and some Scandinavian countries), citizens get to go to college for free.

The point is, in America we have our own bread and circuses. They keep people quiet, compliant, submissive, mollified, politically inactive, and yes, depressed. If a gallon of gasoline or a sixpack of beer cost $25, people would revolt in the streets. But because booze, gas, food, broadband, and other "necessities" of modern life are cheap, we stay numb in our cocoons, oblivious to the very real and injurious injustices of modern life, like the unwitting citizen-dupes in John Carpenter's *They Live*, who go on consuming and obeying, unaware that the aliens have taken control.

Take back control.

Start with your own life.

Start by *recognizing* the mind-control messages, the self-esteem-destroying schemata, of daily life. Then shield yourself from those messages, as best you can. Reject them and begin to live life on *your* terms.

Reject the Comfortable

This may seem counterintuitive. But honestly, you need to stop babying yourself. You need to go outside the comfort zone once in a while. You're spending too much time in the bunker.

Society encourages us to seek comfort at every opportunity. This is the basis of most advertisement. "You're in good hands with Allstate" (Allstate Insurance). "That was easy" (Staples). "It's everywhere you want to be" (Visa). "Have it your way" (Burger King).

It's natural to want to choose comfort over discomfort. I'm not saying to seek discomfort. I'm saying: be open to things that aren't guaranteed to be cozy, familiar, and safe.

It's only when we challenge ourselves, through new experiences, that we can grow, learn, and transform.

People new to psychotherapy often choose a therapist who's "easy to talk to," personable, and fosters a feeling of safety. But comfort is a double-edged sword. If you select a therapist who's too "comfy," too easy to talk to, no real healing is apt to take place.

I hate to be the one to have to tell you this, but personal transformation is about *leaving* your comfort zone, not staying in it.

Yes, you want to feel safe against harm, in a therapeutic setting; that's vital. What you're looking for in a therapist is someone who makes you feel safe about *leaving* your comfort zone, if that makes sense. Therapy is about dealing with sources of discomfort. Sometimes that's painful. That's why every therapist's office has a box of tissues.

Your present coping mechanisms, even if they're harming you, are bringing you some degree of comfort, or you wouldn't cling to them.

Somewhere along the line, though, you have to find new coping tools, techniques that won't bring you more harm than good. That means trying new ways of thinking, new ways of behaving. It means leaving old comforts behind (alcohol, fatty foods, sex, gambling, bad relationships, video games, whatever it happens to be) and finding new comforts; constructive comforts. Venturing into new territory means leaving old habits behind. It means being willing to embrace change. It means going outside what Sting calls "the soul cage." And that's difficult for a lot of people.

You can start by trying something new. Today. Right now. Listen to new music. Watch a TV show you've never watched. Read a book you wouldn't ordinarily read. Go for a walk—and take a new route. Change it up. Whatever you'd usually do, try something different—just once, on a what-the-hell basis.

When old comforts tempt you, say "not now." Write yourself an I.O.U. Agree to let yourself fall back on the old comfort later, some other time; just not now.

The idea isn't to make a wholesale life change. To the contrary, you can start small. The important point is to start.

Start going beyond the comfort zone. It's a zone of stagnation. Remember that the comfort zone is a place of temporary refuge; not a place to live in forever.

Positive Pictures

Do you have pictures—maybe of special places or special people in your life—that bring a warm, positive feeling to you just by looking at them? If not, you need to find some.

Try finding three or four such images. They can be of anything at all that makes you feel good.

Put one picture on your phone (or your iPod Touch); put another on your computer or tablet; put another in a frame, and keep it on your desk or in a place where you can find it easily; keep yet another picture in your purse or wallet.

Several times, throughout the day, look at one (or more) of the pictures. Use the pictures to remind yourself that you still know how to feel positive feelings. Use them to remind yourself that certain things have meaning in your life—a positive meaning.

Change the images every now and then; shuffle them around. Take the one that was in your purse and put in on your phone, or put the phone image on your computer; but switch them around periodically.

Choose images you can look at and say: "This, I know, is good."

These images are antidotes to the toxins in your life. They won't be enough to counter *all* the negative stimuli in your daily life, but they're necessary reminders that life isn't 100% toxic nonsense.

You need those kinds of reminders.

Take Action

Self-esteem is vitally important, and affirmations can help with that, but overall, I'm not a big fan of affirmations, because affirmations can't take the place of action. Action will trump words every time.

Say your goal is to learn French. Imagine how foolish it would be if you chanted to yourself, at various times throughout the day: "I will become fluent in French." "My French will improve daily." "I am good at speaking French." You can say all the affirmations you want, but a trip to France will do more to improve your French than any amount of chanting. If you want to learn French, start watching French movies. Buy some French books. Enroll in a class. Try some online tutorials. The more interactive and action-oriented the option, the better.

You've probably heard the saying "A trip of a thousand miles begins with a single step." The meaning is twofold. First, you won't go anywhere without leaving your house. Secondly, it's not the *size* of the step that matters; what matters is taking the step.

It's important to realize that whatever you goal is, you won't reach it just by reading about it, thinking about it, or sitting at home doing nothing. You need to *take action*. Physical action, if possible.

But it doesn't have to mean dramatic, huge action. To the contrary, it's entirely okay to start small. That's especially true if you feel paralyzed, incapable of doing anything worthwhile.

Suppose you're so depressed, so "covered over" with chores that need to be done and unfinished tasks that need to be finished, that you've let two months' worth of laundry pile up, and as the pile gets bigger, you feel more and more incapable of dealing with it. Each time you look at the dirty laundry, your self-esteem sinks a little lower. You're caught in a downward cycle.

So here's something you can do. The next time you take a shower, bring two laundry items (just two—two undergarments, say) with you into the shower, and wash those items by hand as you shower. Then squeeze them out and hang them up to dry.

By doing this, you immediately prove to yourself that you *can* take action; there *is* hope; and oh by the way, you have clean underwear for tomorrow.

This same technique can be applied to all undone chores in your life. Choose an undone task and commit to doing ten percent of it right now—just *ten percent*. If the sink if full of dirty dishes, do three dishes. If you've got 30 e-mails to answer, answer three. If you have ten bills to pay, pay one.

It may sound ridiculous that you can make serious progress toward a goal by attacking it ten percent at a time, but if you do the math, what you'll find is that ten percent progress toward a goal, every day, gets you more than 100% of the way there after only eight days (if you build on the previous day's progress).

Progress, in life, sometimes happens in big bursts, but more often, it comes in tiny increments. The key is to be persistent and make continual progress toward your goal via small increments.

Suppose (again) your goal is to learn French. Let's say you have only twenty minutes a day to devote to it—an absurdly small amount of time, right? In twenty minutes, you can probably learn ten words. (Make flashcards. Review the words, a few seconds at a time, throughout the day.) After a year, you'll know 3,650 French words. Sure, you'll forget some. Let's say you forget 600. That still leaves you with a vocabulary, after a year's worth of very little daily effort, of more than 3,000 words. That's enough for ordinary conversational French. A five-year-old child has a vocabulary, typically, of around 2,000 to 3,000 words. I don't know about you, but I'd love to be able to speak French (a language I've never studied) at the five-year-old level; to me, it would be a marvelous, thrilling accomplishment, a miracle.

Learning a programming language is a lot like learning a foreign language. Some of it is rote memorization; some of it is syntax; there are idioms to learn; there's logic; there's structure and rules. When I taught myself to program (first in the C language, then Java, and JavaScript), it seemed like there was an awful lot of "wax on, wax off." Remember the scene in *The Karate Kid* where the kid has to wash and wax Mr. Miyagi's car? Miyagi demonstrates the technique, then says (with his inscrutable broken English): "Wax on? Wax off." The Ralph Macchio character reluctantly commits to doing the mindless wax-on/wax-off routine, but grows frustrated, not realizing that he is, in reality, accumulating important "muscle memory" skills that will pay off bigtime later.

Many things in life are like that. You engage in small, incremental, sometimes annoying "wax on, wax off" activities, until one day, finally, it all comes together and you start to see the payoff.

Don't underestimate the importance of small, seemingly insignificant increments of progress. That's how major progress starts.

The important thing is to take action. Make it an absurdly small action, if you want. Make a game out of it; take some action that's comically small. Then give yourself credit. *You took action.*

Do Something Badly

G. K. Chesterton once said "If a thing is worth doing, it's worth doing badly." He was being humorous, of course, but there's also a deep Zen wisdom in what he's saying.

We often fail to do things we need to do because we're afraid we won't do them well enough. When the standard of performance is perfection, there's a huge built-in disincentive that keeps us from acting at all.

Writers know this feeling as "writer's block." Every writer has been blocked at one time or another. Experienced writers know the answer to writer's block: Give yourself permission to write utter crap. Anne Lamott has a chapter in her book *Bird by Bird* called "Shitty First Drafts." The key to writing, Lamott says, is just to begin putting down words, even if they're total junk; just let it out. Make a game of it, if you have to. See how badly you can mangle the language. Try it. Write a lead paragraph, just for your eyes, that's *intentionally* awful. Keep at it and you'll be surprised how liberated you'll start to feel, how quickly the pace picks up.

Every writer (even the best) has written crap. What you have to realize is that, your whole life, all you've ever read in books and magazines and online are final drafts—people's most polished output. *Nothing* you have ever read started out perfect. You didn't see the wadded-up drafts, the false starts, the backspaced-over crap that other authors wrote. You only saw the finished result.

If you engage in something creative, whether it's writing an e-mail or a poem or a novel or a resume, whether it's singing, painting, sculpting, drawing, playing a musical instrument, or whatever, don't censor yourself. Censorship is death to creativity. You can't censor your way to a masterpiece. Don't aim for masterpiece. Only aim to express yourself. Go ahead and be awful. You can always tear it up and start over again. The important point is to *start*.

Start with awfulness, then come back and chip away at the bad parts until the acceptable parts start to become visible, which they eventually will. It's said that Michaelangelo saw, in a piece of marble, that which he wanted to express, and only got to the final work *by removing that which was not needed.* It was a subtractive process.

Your life is a work in progress; a rough draft. Imagine what your life should look like in the next revision. Start by removing that which is not needed.

Intention Deficit Disorder

Much of the time, people who are depressed struggle with agency: the ability to act, the ability to be *proactive*.

You can reinforce your ability to act by focusing more on intentionality. Awareness of intention contributes to a stronger sense of self.

Intention is the glue that cements conscious action to recognition of consequences. When you live without intention, you're at the mercy of forces that seem to tug and pull at you randomly, taking your emotions with them. Call it Intention Deficit Disorder.

By acting with intention, by being mindful of your own sense of what you're trying to do (and what the consequences might be), you can bring greater awareness to whatever you're doing, and achieve desired results more reliably. You will be able to calibrate your actions in a way that brings more meaning into your life. You'll also find it easier to align actions with goals.

Whole books have been written about living with intention, and people have advocated intention-based techniques to build wealth, achieve career success, etc. That's fine. There's nothing wrong with any of that. But that goes beyond what I'm advocating, which is really just a type of mindfulness.

The "success via intention" books say to set goals, make lists, and so on. By all means, do those things, if you want. I'm advocating something much more modest: Start by being aware of your intentions (whatever they are) before you act, and refine your intentions in accordance with desired outcomes; and compare outcomes to intentions.

I don't see living intentionally as an overarching philosophy, necessarily, although there's nothing wrong with that. I see it as a way to live more fully, more effectively, in the *present moment*, which is incredibly important, because too many of us allow ourselves to be weathervaned (and blindsided) by events that seem somehow out of our control. Then we sit there, in the smoking ashes, wondering what the heck just happened.

It's important to recognize *your role* in the things that happen "to you." You'll never do that unless you gain a sense of the importance of intention.

Abdication of personal responsibility is never a good idea. Always recognize your role in whatever happens in your life.

I got a good laugh when I read the part in Steve Chandler's book, *101 Ways to Motivate Yourself*, where he wrote about joining the military, as a young man, to gain self-discipline. When he got to boot camp, he came to a stunning realization. "Somehow," he said, "I had not been aware of the word 'self' in self-discipline." Chandler came to see that no matter what the drill sergeant had him do, he couldn't do it unless *he* willed *himself* to do it. Self-discipline isn't something someone brings you, or forces on you. No drill sergeant can make you do anything you don't want to do.

You have to want to do things. That's intention in action.

Increase your awareness of it and you'll find yourself gaining much-needed clarity.

Act the Part

Most of us are weathervaned by our emotions. All of us are, at times, caught off guard by sudden events; and we react, without thinking. That's normal.

But you also have control over who you want to be, how you want to act.

You have more power over your emotions than you think.

It's partly a matter of practice. Have you *tried* playing a different role? The happy, carefree you may seem like a very different you than you are right now, but it's a role you can slip into or out of, with practice.

In his book *100 Ways to Motivate Yourself* (Career Press, 2004), Steve Chandler talks about the time he enrolled in an acting class, to help him get over "stage fright" so he could be more relaxed when giving presentations and seminars. But he learned something unexpected from acting class. "I learned that my emotions were tools for me to use, not demonic forces," he explains. "I learned that my emotions were mine to work with and change at will."

Chandler found out (as every actor does) that it's possible, when preparing for a role, to draw from deep potentialities in the mind, resources you didn't fully realize were there; mysterious, powerful forces that, with practice, can be summoned—and put to deliberate use.

"It took a great acting teacher, Judy Rollings, and my own long struggles with performing difficult scenes, to show me that my emotions really could be under the complete control of my mind," Chandler says. "I found out that I could motivate myself by thinking and acting like a motivated person, just as I could depress myself by thinking and acting like a depressed person. With practice, the fine line between thinking and acting disappeared."

A serious professional actor *becomes* the character—and we see the result, as brilliant acting. A convincing performance is convincing because it's not *just* a performance. It's reality; a reality of its own.

Does this mean you should consider taking acting lessons? Actually, maybe that's not such a bad idea. Give it some thought. In the meantime, consider what it might take to achieve the kind of absolute control over your emotions that a professional actor has. Think how *useful* that would be, how powerful, how transformative. You have that capacity within you. All it takes is practice, to get in touch with it. It takes practice, and belief, and intent.

Try it right now. Try smiling. Smile as if someone just told you the most absurd, ridiculous joke. Is life too perverse to allow you to smile right now? Smile at the perversity, then, if only to prove you can do it. Smile out of spite! Be an actor, for a moment. For *yourself.* Not to please anyone else.

The "well" you—the future you—is a role. You can start preparing for it now.

Steve Chandler sums it up marvelously: "It doesn't take authentic circumstances to be who you want to be. It just takes rehearsal."

Close the Steel Door

I generally don't buy into easy pop-psych strategies for dealing with serious problems, because they often don't work for me.

But sometimes, some of these easy techniques *do* have utility, and I'd like to mention a couple of them in case they work for *you*. They've occasionally worked for me. (Much to my amazement.)

They involve visualization. *Specific kinds* of visualization.

Visualization can work because the visual parts of your mind are powerful—more powerful than you may think.

I'll give a simple example. Suppose you've been spending too much of your day worrying about a particular issue; maybe bills have piled up or you have an unpleasant chore that needs doing; something's gnawing away at you. It keeps popping into your head, and you can't stop obsessing over it.

As a practical matter, you can't build your day around such thoughts. They get in the way of getting work done.

One thing you can do is set a time limit for thinking about such matters. When the time limit is up, you put the thoughts away, with the promise to return to them later, at a more appropriate time. But here's how you put them away: You close your eyes, clear your mind, and picture a *gigantic metal vault*, like the kind you see at some banks. The worries you have, the problems, the bills, the laundry, whatever it happens to be, are on a metal cart. You wheel the metal cart to the open door of the vault and *shove* the cart in; it coasts into the vault. Then you slam the humongous freakin' stainless steel door on the vault and turn the huge handle that lock the door shut. The metal cart is no longer visible; it's in the vault, out of sight, where it will stay until you decide to return to it.

Notice before, I said you are putting the thoughts away with a promise to return to them later. This aspect (of promising to return later) is important, because it means you're not denying the existence of the problems, or the fact that you will attend to them. *Denying* a problem's existence is futile. Telling yourself you'll *never get to it* is counterproductive, because it leads to a sense of defeat, a loss of self-esteem, a lack of agency. Don't beat yourself up that way. Don't test your willpower, because that just leads to self-punishment. Defuse your sense of defeat by admitting to yourself that you *do* still have the problem, and you will, in fact, get to it, *just not right this minute*. Because you have other things to do.

If you find that visualization tricks of this sort are useful, you might want to experiment with a few others.

Suppose you've decided to give in to an urge to eat a chocolate bar that you know you shouldn't eat. After your first bite, or maybe your second bite (relish those bites, by the way), stop. Imagine, for a moment, that you've just been told—in fact, you can see for yourself —that the bar is tainted with dog poop. Have you ever taken a Baby Ruth bar out of its wrapper and laid it on a table? It looks like a goddam dog poop. When I was young, I used to take a Baby Ruth bar (minus wrapper) and stick it in my younger brother's bed, just to scare the hell out of him, because I knew he'd think it was dog poop.

Once you get it in your mind that you might be eating dog poop, you'll find it easier to defer the eating of the rest of that candy bar.

Be as gross as you want with your visualizations. When you're halfway through a cigarette, imagine that it feel on the ground in a puddle of cat pee. Put the cigarette out. You only needed the first couple of puffs anyway.

That extra helping of pizza you're trying to avoid? It's covered with vomit. It even smells funny. Don't touch it.

Be creative. Come up with your own visualizations, that work for you. You may be surprised to find that some *do, in fact, work.*

To List or Not to List?

I have a confession to make: I have a love-hate relationship with lists.

I'm reluctant to give any list-oriented tips in this book, because I know, from personal experience, not everyone finds list-making (and crossing things off a list) useful.

I see a list and am immediately concerned that I won't get to everything on the list. The idea of not completing a list concerns me, because I'm one of those people who hates to leave anything undone. If I start reading a book, I feel compelled to finish it. (If it's a bad book and I don't finish it, I feel bad for not finishing it.) If I start eating a salad, or a cookie, or an apple, I have to finish it. If I start watching a movie, I have to finish it. If I start washing dishes, I have to do them all.

So if I see a list, my immediate worry is that not everything on the list will get checked off. And that's a problem. I can't leave something half-done.

Instead of putting tasks into list form, I prefer a strategy of handling every task as soon as I encounter it. If an e-mail arrives and I'm not sure what to do with it, I have to choose, immediately, between dealing with it *later* and dealing with it *now*; I always deal with it *now*, because otherwise I know I'll never get to it. The same is true of physical mail. When mail arrives in the (outdoor) mailbox, I have to go through it quickly, piece by piece, right away. Because otherwise it will sit in a stack of unread mail for weeks or months.

If someone hands me a rough draft of a document and says "Take a look at this when you have a moment; you can get back to me on it tomorrow," I start looking at it right away so I can get it off my desk and not worry about it later.

When it comes to *starting* a task, I'll sometimes procrastinate. But once I do start, I have to finish.

Handling tasks immediately is a good solution for me, but I recognize it's not workable for everybody. Some people do better with making *lists* of tasks that need attention, and working the tasks off one by one until the list is done.

I do recognize the importance of lists, because as a pilot, I'm well accustomed to dealing with checklists. Checklists are extraordinarily important, especially in the context of an inflight emergency. A checklist keeps you focused; it forces you to stay prioritized; it forces you to attend to important items one by one, in a predetermined order; and it ensures you'll do a complete job—you won't overlook something important (which you might, if you're *not* going by a checklist).

But even in aviation, it's possible to do without lists.

One day, I had an opportunity to fly copilot with a close acquaintance, in a high-performance airplane (a Mitsubishi MU-2F propjet). For whatever reason, my friend couldn't locate the plane's checklists; they weren't where they were supposed to be that day. We had our navigation charts, but no checklists. I assumed he'd cancel the flight. Not so.

To my amazement, Roger decided to go ahead with the flight. His decision stunned me, frankly, because this was an extremely sophisticated airplane with a complicated instrument panel, with *many* switches, gauges, annunciator lights, circuit breakers, fuel selector valves, radios, autopilot systems, backup systems, and so on. It was like a small airliner. I knew that Roger was a very experienced professional pilot (he had flown Ford Motor Company executives around, in a previous job; and had flown cargo planes in the Air Force), but still—how could he be sure of doing a safe job *without a checklist?*

Roger showed me his technique, which was to work his way around the cockpit, systematically, item by item, looking at and *touching* (with his fingertips) *every* instrument, switch, lever, knob, etc., in the cockpit (and in the overhead panel, and side panels). Each time he touched something, he said the item's name aloud and recited its proper condition (which he knew by heart), then verified that the knob, switch, dial, or control in question *was, in fact, set* to the correct setting. He did this before engine start, and again before takeoff, and again before landing. I observed carefully, to see if he'd overlook anything. He never did.

I learned something important from that experience, which is that by being methodical, systematic, and thorough, using *all* your senses —being *mindful, intentional,* and *in the moment*—you can get through even a dauntingly complex job without making a mistake.

Lists are great tools for maintaining focus, prioritizing tasks, marking progress, and ensuring thoroughness. Use them, if you're a "list" kind of person. But also realize, there are other strategies that can work just as well.

Be Here Now

When depression grinds you down, you tend to block out the world, as much as possible. Every external stimulus seems to add to the sensory overload. You begin to shut down. In reality, you need to let the sunlight in.

Start by living in the present moment. That means shutting out the past and the future. There's a time for worry (about the future) and guilt, regret, and anger (things that happened in the past), but you shouldn't allow those things to consume you to the point where you can't live in the present moment.

Sir Walter Scott said he'd trade years of mindless conformity for "*one hour* of life crowded to the full with glorious action and filled with noble risks."

You'll know you've reached the apex of living in the here-and-now when you begin to realize that conscious well-being—what people call "happiness"—is not some nebulous thing that's *out there* somewhere. It's all right here. Heaven, hell, and everything in between can be found in the present moment.

Stop looking "out there." The solution to your problems isn't in a pill at the pharmacy or on a shelf somewhere in WalMart; it's not going to come in a box from Amazon. Happiness isn't something you find in a therapist's office or at the mall or in a park or zoo or library. It's not something you magically stumble upon at a Zen retreat, or in a yoga class. It's not your favorite Disneyland ride. It's everywhere, all the time.

It's said that in America, we try to cultivate an appreciation of art, whereas the Japanese cultivate the art of appreciation. It's a subtle but fundamental difference of outlook.

I know very little about Zen (even after reading Alan Watts), but it amazes me that even with my limited knowledge of it, I know enough to know you don't have to go looking for it in monasteries or classes. Zen isn't "out there." It's right here, right now. If there's a secret to Zen, that's pretty much it. Few Americans seem to get it.

When you begin to practice mindfulness, you'll find yourself sleeping better. If you don't believe me, try a simple experiment. At the end of the day, a half hour to an hour before you go to bed, finish your chores, turn off the TV and the music, turn the lights low, and read a book, meditate, or draw. Do something to quiet your mind. Finally, before going to bed, just sit. For five minutes. Let the buzz in your head wind down. Be here now, in the present moment. Don't reflect, don't judge, don't fret. Look at a peaceful image, or close your eyes and visualize a pleasant image, and let your brain "exhale."

If you do this for a few nights in a row, pretty soon you'll be going to sleep faster and sleeping better.

Contrast this with what a lot of people do. Many people finish up a few last-minute chores (maybe in the kitchen), turn the music (or the TV) off, brush teeth, turn the lights out, then hop right in bed—and start tossing and turning, unable to settle down.

But look at what's going on. Throughout the day, your mind fills with concerns of the day; you stimulate your brain further with TV or Internet; you rush through a few last-minute chores; then you turn the lights out and get in bed, where it's dead-quiet (and dark). The sudden sensory deprivation allows the thoughts swirling in your head to come to the fore, blaring, demanding to be heard (which they will be, with lights off and silence in the house). All of a sudden, your head is the noisiest thing in the room.

This is why insomnia is so common in depression. When there's nothing else to listen to but your own thoughts, those thoughts start to take over. Pretty soon it's two in the morning and you're reaching for the sleeping pills. Or you get up and watch some TV and try the whole cycle all over again.

Try living in the present moment *while you're awake*, so you don't have to fight your own thoughts when you lie down at night.

If you're living with *intention*, you'll plan your day (and evening) to follow a certain trajectory that agrees with how your mind works. For me, that means watching TV only up to a certain hour, then downgrading to a book (or soothing music) for a while, then downgrading to peace and quiet, *then* going to bed. If I'm going to pay bills or do chores or engage in something that makes me crazy, I try to get that out of the way *well* before bedtime. I don't just turn the lights off and magically expect my brain to go to sleep.

It's not rocket science. It's common sense.

Live in the present moment. Set limits for yourself when it comes to fixating on the future or the past. When the time limit is up, it's up: Cut yourself an I.O.U. Promise yourself you'll get back to worrying or fixating on the past (or whatever) *tomorrow*. In the meantime, now is now. Spend more time in the here-and-now.

Help Your Therapist Out

If you're seeing a therapist, you should know that that person is not clairvoyant. Big shock, right?

But it's amazing how many people go into a therapy session and fail to convey their concerns openly, transparently, to their therapist. Lots of small talk happens; you update the therapist on how your life is going; but somehow, overall, you end up conveying the impression that you're doing better than you really are. Maybe it's your way of fostering optimism. *I'm making progress*, you might be thinking to yourself. *Things aren't really so bad.*

A good therapist will, of course, try to draw you out and get past the superficial talk, to the things that *need* to be discussed. But the point is, your therapist is not superhuman. He or she is not clairvoyant. That person can't possibly know what's *really* bothering you until you bring it up. If you hide behind a facade of normalcy, you're cheating yourself. You're wasting time.

Help your therapist out.

Make it clear what's bothering you, giving you trouble. Give your therapist the necessary clues.

Until you get the hang of this, it may help to write your concerns down ahead of time. Keep a notebook going. Make a list and update it between therapy visits. Bring notes. Then speak up.

Our culture values the idea of outsourcing, the notion that you can hire an expert to take care of problems for you, whether it's getting your car fixed or paying someone to dry-clean your clothes or whatever. But don't carry that notion into therapy. You're not handing your psyche to someone with the demand: Here, fix this for me. Are you? Because that's not how it works.

Therapy is a two-way street. Meet your therapist halfway. Get to the the painful stuff right away. Don't dance around it. You're the one paying—for the therapy, and for the psychic pain that results if you don't get the things done that need to get done.

Suffering and Progress

It's fairly well accepted in psychiatric circles that depression patients, once they begin therapy (whether it's drug therapy or talk therapy, or both), can often get worse before getting better.

This was already well known as long ago as 1960. If you look, for example, at Slater and Roth's *Clinical Psychiatry*, by Bailliere, Tindall and Cassell (London, 1960), p. 231, you'll find the statement:

> With beginning convalescence (following initiation
> of treatment with tricyclic antidepressants), the
> risk of suicide once more becomes serious as
> retardation fades.

This was standard medical-textbook knowledge, in the 1960s. It used to be called the "roll-back phenomenon."

Be on guard for it.

Various mechanisms have been proposed for the increase in suicidality early in treatment of depression:

- **Activation:** This view holds that antidepressants with prominent energizing effects can actually increase suicidal behavior in severely depressed patients whose psychomotor retardation was (in the absence of therapy) keeping them in a lethargic, avolitional state. Untreated, their own stupor inhibited such patients from acting out their suicidal thoughts.

- **Paradoxical worsening of depression:** This is the view

that, in some patients, depressed moods may actually *worsen* as a direct result of antidepressant treatment. We know that this does, in fact, happen in some patients, for some drugs.

• **Akathisia:** This idea holds that some antidepressants produce a side effect of akathisia[17], which is known to be associated with suicide risk. Note that akathisia is actually a complex syndrome with mood, mentation, and motor components. It's far more than just "restless legs" or "restlessness," although people have often confused it with mere restlessness.

• **Anxiety:** This is the view that certain antidepressants may induce anxiety and panic attacks, which can lead to suicidal behavior in certain patients. (There is reason to believe, however, that many clinicians have recorded a patient's reports of "anxiety" without considering whether the anxiety was actually reflective of akathisia.)

• **Stage shifts:** This is the view that antidepressants may cause a switch from depression into mixed states or a bipolar-like condition. Bipolar illness is known to be associated with very high rates of suicidality. The use of antidepressants does bring a risk of mood switch, even in unipolar patients.

---

17 Akathisia is a complex syndrome, characterized by "extrapyramidal effects" (motor or muscle dysfunction of various kinds), agitation, dysphoria (feeling ill at ease, "feeling wrong"), and/or suicidality. Many types of drugs (including but not limited to antidepressants and antipsychotics) can bring this reaction in a minority of patients. When it occurs, it's serious and requires immediate professional intervention. Read more about this important disorder at http://asserttrue.blogspot.com/2015/01/the-curse-of-akathisia.html (retrieved 2 Feb. 2015).

- **Insomnia:** This view says that insomnia associated with certain antidepressants may lead to suicidal behavior in some patients.

The last point (insomnia) doesn't make much sense until you realize that suicide rates (when analyzed by time of day) reach their peak at 2:00 to 2:59 a.m.[18]

I believe good evidence exists for all of the mechanisms proposed above. The "activation" explanation is quite old and has been relied on by many clinicians to explain rollback.

The fact is, though, that once you begin to bring up painful issues in therapy—and begin confronting them in a realistic manner—it can be disorienting, heightening your sense of distress. It's paradoxical, because you go to therapy expecting to *feel better.* In point of fact, working on difficult issues is hard, and you may very well feel worse before you feel better.

Be ready for it. And try not to let it dishearten you. If you come out of a therapy session in tears, retraumatized, it may actually be a sign of progress.

---

18 See http://www.uphs.upenn.edu/news/News_Releases/2014/06/perlis/ (retrieved 2 Feb. 2015).

The Pleasure Principle

Anhedonia, which is the fancy medical word for an inability to experience pleasure, is a signature hallmark of depression. In fact, if you check the DSM's diagnostic criteria for Major Depressive Episode, you have to have either anhedonia or a marked depression of mood, or both, to qualify for a diagnosis of major depression.

As a practical matter, severe depression almost always comes with anhedonia, and it's known, also, that anhedonia is extremely common in Parkinson's disease, probably a consequence of the abnormal dopamine processing in that disease.

The medical literature on anhedonia is vast, highly technical, and generally unhelpful, because to this day, no drug has been approved specifically for treating anhedonia, even though there's a pressing need for such drugs, and even though we know dopamine agonists (Parkinson's drugs) tend to be somewhat effective in this regard. There are many anecdotal accounts in online forums of Parnate (tranylcypromine), a monoamine oxidase inhibitor, being helpful for anhedonia, but aside from that, it's hard to find evidence of anything other than stimulants being helpful.[19]

If you've never experienced anhedonia, count yourself lucky. It's thoroughly awful. It means you can't read a book, enjoy music (or a movie), enjoy sex, or appreciate any of the big *or* small pleasures of life. It's known to be one of the main reasons heroin users can't

19 There is some evidence that the anesthetic ketamine is useful for anhedonia (it is also useful in emergency treatment of suicidal depression), but it must be administered by an anesthesiologist at a hospital. See http://www.nature.com/tp/journal/v4/n10/full/tp2014105a.html (retrieved 3 Feb. 2015) for a recent study reporting ketamine's anti-anhedonia effects.

readjust well to life without heroin. (Cocaine withdrawal, likewise.) Life just goes from color to black and white, and you feel emotionally tone deaf.

Unfortunately, selective serotonin reuptake inhibitors (SSRIs like Prozac and Zoloft), and norepinephrine reuptake inhibitors (SNRIs, like Effexor and Pristiq) often have the effect of blunting people's pleasure response, aggravating anhedonia. You end up, sometimes, feeling numbed out; maybe not exactly zombie-like, but flat—apathetic to otherwise-pleasurable activities.

Complain about it to your doctor. If the drugs are making you worse off than before, maybe add Abilify (which is not going to help much with depression, but is at least a partial dopamine agonist) or experiment with an older drug, such as Parnate.

You could also try going to a *neurologist*, someone who treats Parkinson's patients, and explain your anhedonia symptoms, and say that you've heard that dopamine agonists can be helpful for anhedonia (which is what the literature suggests).

Failing that, you could consult with your clinician about the possibility of going off antidepressants entirely. It depends how bad your anhedonia is, and whether drugs made it worse. If your depression has faded (with the help of antidepressants), but you're unable to feel your emotions any more, is that better, or worse, than being depressed? That's something only you can decide.

I tried a wide variety of SSRIs and SNRIs, with and without so-called "mood stabilizers" (Depakote, Lamictal). The latter were placebos, to me. They did nothing. (My wife has also taken "mood stabilizers"; they did absolutely nothing.) The SSRIs and SNRIs blunted my sexuality and made my emotional availability go flatline. As soon as I went off the drugs, I felt better.

That doesn't mean you have to give up on antidepressants totally. SSRIs and SNRIs aren't the only game in town. There are also serotonergic non-SSRI drugs like Remeron (which worked for me) and older tricyclics and tetracyclics, plus the MAO inhibitors. The

MAOIs have largely fallen out of favor because of the arcane dietary restrictions they necessitate, but they're worthwhile drugs.

This is a discussion for you and your doctor to have. So have it. Don't just accept anhedonia forever. Demand more out of life. Demand to know what your options are, and keep trying different things until you find a combination that works.

Add Structure

I mentioned, in an earlier chapter, the value of balance—the importance of not letting major elements of your life go *out* of balance. Spending too much time, thought, or emotional energy on any one thing is rarely a good idea. That's just common sense.

But there's also such a thing as maintaining *structure* in your life. There's some overlap here with the idea of balance, but really, structure is a topic of its own, and it's incredibly important, so I want to elaborate on it for a moment.

In my book *Of Two Minds*, I talk about my personal experience in mental health rehab and what it was like. I was in "the mental ward" twice: once for suicidal tendencies, once for a mixed diagnosis of depression and alcohol abuse. Each stay was ten nights (eleven days) long. I improved tremendously, and I saw the vast majority of other patients improve dramatically as well, when I went through the "program." The components of the program were straightforward. It involved:

1. Complete isolation from the concerns of the outside world. No computers, phones, e-mail, etc.
2. Adherence to "three square meals a day" (rather than *ad libitum* eating of random snacks, junk food, and so on).
3. Zero alcohol.
4. Zero caffeine.
5. Highly structured daily routine.
6. Complete change-up of meds.
7. Regular sleep schedule.

8. Some exposure to exercise (although this was *not* pushed aggressively on anyone).

9. Frequent face-to-face social interaction with live humans.

10. Daily access to a psychiatrist (albeit for no more than 10 minutes).

11. Daily access to group therapy.

12. Extremely limited access to TV.

13. Extremely limited access to a phone.

14. Frequent access to tobacco, if you wanted it.

The final item on the list may seem odd. There were frequent "smoke breaks" for those who wished to smoke cigarettes. The idea being, you're under enough stress already, without adding the psychic (and physical) symptoms of tobacco withdrawal; therefore, work on the things you're there to work on, first, *then* worry about smoking cessation later, when you have some coping skills.

There are many synergies hidden in the above list. Sequestration from the outside world cuts down on sources of stress, but also forces you to spend more time dealing, face to face, with live humans (because you're not on the Internet, at all, *ever*, in the ward). You get to eat three meals a day, on schedule. But there's little opportunity for between-meals snacking. Your TV time is severely limited. This helps with maintaining your hunger at meal time. Why? Because most Americans eat something (popcorn, chips, candy, "fun food") while watching TV, and studies show that the more you watch TV while you eat, the bigger portions you eat of whatever you're eating. Many people like to drink wine or beer while watching TV, too. You'll do none of that in the ward. For once, you'll watch an hour of TV and not be constantly pushing food (or beer) into your mouth.

Some people like to eat or drink while talking on the phone. Guess what? In lockup, you don't get to talk on the phone, except maybe once a day for five minutes. And you won't be eating or drinking when you're doing it.

It's funny how, when you begin to adhere to a few simple structural constraints, so many bad habits fall by the wayside. You don't even know it's happening.

My humble suggestion to you is that if you're not eating right (or not eating on any kind of schedule; you're eating whatever you want, whenever you want, while you're watching TV or surfing the Web or talking on the phone); your social life is out of balance (because you're either not socializing with people, or you're socializing with the *wrong* people); you're drinking a little too much; you're not adhering to a *precise* medication regimen; you have haphazard sleep hours; you have no daily schedule; your daily life lacks structure; then you need to consider getting your daily life in order. On your own. Today. Because you want to. Because you *need* to.

The alternative is: You can wait until you need an intervention—and end up having the aforementioned "structure" *imposed on you*. Some people do need that. And there's nothing wrong with that. Just realize, *you can do it now, on your own—or you can have it imposed on you later.* It's something to think about.

It may sound incredibly simplistic to think imposing a little structure on your daily life can have a big payoff. But it's not so hard to believe, really. It works. I promise. I've seen what it does. And I've seen what *lack* of structure does.

Try the structured approach. It costs nothing, and it may keep you out of the mental ward, where structure is the name of the game.

Compliance

Meds compliance is hard. I've diddled with my meds over the years; I know what that's about. When you're in a desperate state, you'll try all kinds of things: going up or down on meds, skipping meds one day, doubling up the next, etc. Pretty soon, you become disgusted with meds, in general. You become convinced they're useless.

What you need to do, though, before giving up on meds, is adhere to a strict schedule (and a rigidly consistent dosage) for at least two weeks. Otherwise, with so many variables in play (particularly if you're eating irregularly, sleeping irregularly, drinking alcohol, etc.), you won't really have any idea what the meds are (or aren't) doing for you. You need to establish a baseline. That means *consistency*—in as many variables as you can control. After two weeks of taking meds in the prescribed amount, at a fixed time every day, if they aren't working —fine. They aren't working. *Then* you can consider a new plan of action. *But not until then.*

Tweaking, adjusting, diddling with meds is tempting. But it leads to an out-of-control cycle. You may find that a "meds holiday" of a few days actually makes you feel better; so you decide (prematurely and inappropriately) to just stay off them for a while. Before you know it, you're feeling strange withdrawal effects—and decide to go back on the meds. But now it's going to take a day or two (or three or six) for your blood levels to come back up.

Take it from me. I've been there. And I have many friends who've been there. The thing to do is try strict compliance (and I do mean strict; take your meds at the same time each day) for two weeks, minimum. Establish a baseline. Observe how you are. Get a feel for what the drugs are or aren't doing. Keep a notebook, if you have to.

It may well turn out the drugs aren't right for you. But you won't know that for sure without establishing a baseline.

Get the baseline results first. *Then* make adjustments (but keep your clinician in the loop).

The alternative, believe me, is chaos.

No More Alcohol

Second only to sugar and caffeine, alcohol is the most widely used substance with which people self-medicate. People use it for a variety of reasons. Anxiety control is one of the chief reasons. It's also good at "turning the volume down" on the outside world. People who suffer from depression often find themselves hypersensitized to disagreeable external stimuli, whether it's light, noise, other people, or whatever. Sometimes you feel like you need to blunt those stimuli. Alcohol is good at that.

You should know that substance abuse (of which alcohol abuse is merely a specific example) goes hand in hand with and mood disorders. One study found that people with a mental disorder are 2.7 times more likely to engage in substance abuse.[20] A recent review of the associations between alcohol use disorders (AUD) and major depression (MD) found that the presence of either disorder more than doubled the risk of having the other disorder.[21] The review's authors said: "The current state of the literature suggests a *causal linkage* between alcohol use disorders and major depression, such that increasing involvement with alcohol increases risk of depression."

I drank my first beer in 1966. I took alcohol out of my life in 2012. So what's that? Almost fifty years of drinking? I wish I had some of that time, money, and health back now.

I learned how to drink from my dad, who was an expert drinker, by

---

20 Regier, D.A. et al. (1990), " Comorbidity of Mental Disorders With Alcohol and Other Drug Abuse: Results From the Epidemiologic Catchment Area (ECA) Study," *JAMA* 1990, 264(19):2511-2518.

21 Boden, J.M. and Fergusson, D.M. (2011), "Alcohol and Depression," *Addiction* 106:5, 906-914

which I mean he never got sloppy drunk; he drank mostly beer, mostly in moderation; and I never saw him black out, lose his temper, get in trouble with the law, miss a day of work, etc. because of drinking. He was a "model drunk," if you will. Maybe *drunk* is too harsh a word. He was a *heavy drinker.*

What, exactly, is a "heavy drinker"? According to the Substance Abuse and Mental Health Services Administration (SAMHSA), an agency of the U.S. Department of Health and Human Services, *heavy drinking* is the consumption of five or more drinks on the same occasion (in the "same session") on each of five or more days in the past 30 days.

By that definition, I was a heavy drinker for at least 20 years.

Then, in 2012, my depression got so bad, and my life so out of control, that I went into the mental ward (actually, a small mental health rehab hospital in Jacksonville, Florida) for eleven days. I tell the story of that in my book *Of Two Minds*.

When I got out, I was no longer a drinker.

I never buy alcohol any more. I don't miss it at all. Never have a craving. I think I just drank and drank and drank for so many years that I finally reached a point where I'd had enough. The positive effects no longer outweighed the negative. I wasn't getting the buzz I'd come to depend on; the alcohol was *impairing* me but not *improving* me, in any way whatsoever.

Like all problem drinkers, I resisted (vigorously) the notion that I had a problem. The notion that I was alcohol-*dependent* seemed absurd. Yet the fact remained, I couldn't go a day without a beer. Oh sure, I skipped a day here and there—when I was too hungover to drink. The thought of going a *week* or more without beer, however, was repugnant, untenable, unthinkable.

And yeah, I knew (because everybody tells you this) that alcohol is a depressant. It has mood effects, not merely sedation effects. Still, I downplayed the effects, because beer, for me, *was* therapy (in a weird way). It was a tool for keeping reality at bay.

William Burroughs, author of *Naked Lunch* and *Junky*, was a bigtime drug addict. Late in his life, he discovered something. "There isn't any feeling you can get on drugs," he said, "that you can't get without drugs."

That's quite a statement, coming from one of the most celebrated heroin addicts of the twentieth century.

After decades of drinking, I found that alcohol was giving me no moods, feelings, insights, or "highs" that I couldn't get in other ways. It had lost its ability to do anything positive for me. And yet I clung to it, unable to go without it—out of sheer habit.

How about you? Can *you* go a week without a drink? Seriously. If you can't go a week without a drink, stop and consider the reality of what that means. It means alcohol is a problem. It means you're *dependent* on it. How can it mean anything else?

I resisted going off alcohol, even though my mind told me abstinence was the right thing to do. I needed help to get away from it. I got that help—and now I'm free.

I never considered myself an *alcoholic* (even though I was clearly dependent), for two reasons: First, I never had withdrawal symptoms (such as delirium tremens). My body wasn't *that* addicted to alcohol. But secondly, I refused (and still refuse) to buy into the Alcoholics Anonymous myth that once you admit you're alcohol-dependent, you're stuck with a lifelong disease.

The Alcoholics Anonymous conception of alcoholism as disease is a dangerous one, because it condemns people to a lifelong self-esteem problem from which there is no escape. It forecloses the possibility of being cured. That's a possibility you should never take away from *anyone*.

But also, I disagree with the A.A. conception of alcohol dependence as a *disease*. Alcoholics Anonymous didn't invent the idea of alcohol dependence as disease (that idea had a long history, before A.A. came on the scene), but A.A. did actively push the concept, in the 1950s, as a way to reduce stigma. And it succeeded in doing that. Nonetheless, while there are parallels between alcohol dependence and physical disease (namely: physical symptoms, convalescence, recovery), that doesn't *make* it a true disease, like measles. Sure, you can develop a diseased liver from drinking too much; that's a disease condition. But alcohol dependence, in and of itself, is not a disease any more than coffee dependence is a disease.

It's interesting to compare and contrast cigarette dependence and alcohol dependence. No one questions that tobacco, like alcohol, becomes highly addictive for certain individuals. Yet there is no "disease" in the *Diagnostic and Statistical Manual* called nicotinism or Tobacco Use Syndrome, analogous to alcoholism. We don't speak of tobacco users as being *ill* with an incurable disease that requires they live "one day at a time." Alcohol dependency has been enshrined with "disease" status, whereas smokers are merely ordinary people who've made a bad health choice. If an alcoholic relapses, it's the disease's fault. If a smoker relapses, he made a decision to start smoking again. An alcoholic is ultimately powerless and must give himself over to a Higher Power in order to get better (according to Alcoholics Anonymous); but even then, he remains an alcoholic forever. A smoker, on the other hand, can become a non-smoker—then walk away from the label "smoker," a whole person again.

I prefer to think of alcohol dependency as a habit, born of choice. Like smokers, drinkers can give up their habit—their drug of choice— and become whole again (although some people will need a great deal of help with this). Nevertheless: You have a choice. You can *make decisions* about your health. You can exert control over your fate. The old-fashioned "disease" model of alcoholism takes away choice, hope, and agency; it makes people cripples. I say reject all that. Just reject it.

When I came out of the hospital, something amazing happened. *I found I was no longer bipolar.* For about a month, I had no depression whatsoever. When it finally reappeared, it was of a different quality, greatly attenuated, not overpowering; I *struggled*, but not in a life-or-death way. Somehow, I had acquired a different perspective, a new kind of objectivity, that allowed me to weigh my options and think things through in a clear state of mind (or *clearer*, at least). The low-grade depression that came over me lingered (and thus is properly categorized as *dysthymia*). But it wasn't *crippling*. I could move forward, under my own power.

I also lost a bit of weight. (Shocking, right?) I was no longer consuming 1600 calories a day from an aluminum can. As my weight went down, *my mood went up*. Coincidence? I don't think so.

Something like this may happen to you, if you cut alcohol out of your life. You'll lose weight, gain energy, think more clearly, have a bit more self-esteem, feel less depressed; all important advantages (wouldn't you say?) for a person dealing with depression.

Alcoholics Anonymous works for many people, but it's not for everyone. If you're not familiar with the 12 Steps, most of them involve God in one way or another; the Alcoholics Anonymous program is basically a form of faith healing. Mind you, faith healing does work for some people. The rest of us need something different.

"Something different" can include things like:

- Self Management and Recovery Training, SMART (http://www.smartrecovery.org/intro/)
- Harm Reduction for Alcohol, HAMS (http://www.hamsnetwork.org/)
- My Way Out (http://www.mywayout.org/)
- Moderation Management (http://moderation.org/)
- Secular Organizations for Sobriety, SOS (http://www.sossobriety.org/home.html)
- LifeRing, an offshoot of SOS (http://lifering.org/)
- Rational Recovery (https://rational.org/index.php?id=1)

Most of these approaches feature face-to-face meeting groups and online forums and chat rooms. Rational Recovery was founded by Jack Trimpey and was originally a support group. Trimpey later decided that support groups were an addiction in and of themselves, and disbanded the RR support groups, some of which then became

SMART Recovery groups. HAMS recommends Trimpey's *The Small Book* (Rational Recovery Systems, 1995[22]) as having many useful tips for people seeking to achieve abstinence.

My recommendation is that if you are self-medicating with alcohol, try an alcohol fast (assuming you're not addicted) and see if it helps with your depression. If you're addicted, don't be afraid to seek help. There are *many* kinds of help; A.A. is not the only game in town.

Alcohol isn't helping you, believe me. One drink, now and then, won't kill you (and may even extend your life), but anything beyond that is asking for trouble, if you're depressed. For the longest time, I refused to believe that. Then I tried abstinence—and found my world changing for the better.

Try the experiment for yourself. Try giving up alcohol. Then record your experiences; observe yourself. You may begin to see things (including traumatic things, unfortunately) more clearly. But that's often the first step in dealing with problems. You can't deal effectively with problems when you're in a muddled state of mind.

---

22 http://www.amazon.com/gp/product/0440507251/ref=as_li_tl?
ie=UTF8&camp=1789&creative=9325&creativeASIN=0440507251&linkCode=
as2&tag=asse0a-20&linkId=YBXRYIZO45QFYWQC (retrieved 8 Jan. 2015)

Coffee Is Your Friend

Very few drugs can be shown, convincingly, to be associated with a definite reduction in suicide rate. Scientists have tried to show this for antidepressants, but it isn't an easy connection to demonstrate. There are too many confounding factors.

To my knowledge, only two drugs seem to show a consistent, believable connection with reduced suicide rate: lithium (widely prescribed for bipolar disorder) and caffeine.

Lithium's tendency to prevent suicide in high-risk groups (like bipolar patients) is fairly well known, and the literature on this is extensive. (You can read more about it in my book *Of Two Minds*.) It's extraordinarily cheap and effective, can be taken as-needed (because it works quickly), and is reasonably safe as long as you drink lots of fluids and don't exceed the toxic dose. Unfortunately, "therapeutic grade" lithium carbonate is only available by prescription (in the U.S.), and doctors are still using 50-year-old dosage guidelines that call for dangerously high (toxic) doses of the stuff: 900 mg or more a day. However, you can find lithium orotate or lithium aspartate online or in select health food stores (in dosages that are far lower and more appropriate). You might want to look into that for mood control.

Caffeine (in the form of coffee) is also, potentially, a powerful aid for maintaining mental health. The scientific results for caffeine are correlational; they do not prove cause and effect. Still, the evidence is intriguing. In 2011, Michel Lucas *et al.* published a study in *JAMA Internal Medicine*[23] that looked at 50,739 U.S. women (mean age: 63

---

23 Lucas *et al.* (2011), "Coffee, Caffeine, and Risk of Depression Among Women," *Arch Intern Med.* (now *JAMA Internal Medicine*) 2011;171(17):1571-1578.

years) who were free of depressive symptoms at baseline (in 1996), then prospectively followed up through June 1, 2006. During 10 years of follow-up (1996-2006), 2,607 incident cases of depression were identified. The researchers went back over the data for coffee consumption. They found that depression risk decreases with increasing caffeinated coffee consumption. What's more, they found a clear dose-response relationship. The relative risk was 0.85 (95% confidence interval, 0.75-0.95) for those consuming 2 to 3 cups per day and 0.80 (0.64-0.99; P for trend <.001) for those consuming 4 cups per day or more. In plain English, that means a risk reduction of 15% for drinkers of 2 to 3 cups of coffee per day and 20% risk reduction for those drinking more than that.

Lucas followed up two years later with an expanded study that looked specifically at *suicide* risk among coffee drinkers.[24] In this study, Lucas *et al.* analyzed data for 43,599 men and 164,825 women, covering a period of 20 years for men (14 to 16 years for women), and found a strong dose-dependent inverse association between coffee consumption and suicide, with the risk of suicide 45% reduced for drinkers of 2 to 3 cups per day and 53% reduced for drinkers of more than 4 cups of coffee a day. The researchers corrected for a variety of potential confounding factors, including smoking, antidepressant use, alcohol consumption, age, gender, and marital status. (Read the study to get the full discussion.) Neither tea nor decaffeinated coffee conferred any risk reduction.

The Lucas results confirm two earlier studies. A 1993 study showed lower suicide risk among coffee drinkers in a longitudinal investigation of over 120,000 individuals who were followed for an average of 8 years.[25] Suicide risk decreased monotonically with

---

doi:10.1001/archinternmed.2011.393.

24 Lucas et al. (2014), "Coffee, caffeine, and risk of completed suicide: results from three prospective cohorts of American adults," *World J Biol Psychiatry.* 2014 Jul;15(5):377-86. Doi: 10.3109/15622975.2013.795243.

25 Klatsky A.L., Armstrong M.A., Friedman G.D. (1993), "Coffee, tea, and mortality," *Ann Epidemiol.* 1993 Jul;3(4):375-81.

increasing coffee consumption, and was 80% lower in drinkers of six cups of coffee per day as compared to non-coffee-drinkers.

Likewise, a 1996 study involving 86,626 female nurses found suicide risk was 72% lower among women who drank four cups of caffeinated coffee per day as compared to non-drinkers during the first 10 years of follow-up.[26]

Before you get too excited, bear in mind that a research team in Finland found, in 2000, that suicide risk is 58% *greater* in people who drink eight cups or more of coffee per day.[27] One can hypothesize that agitation, anxiety, and impulsivity (all of which are likelier if you ingest too much caffeine) may be important effects here. But there are other possible explanations, including the likelihood that people who feel the need to self-medicate with 8+ cups of coffee a day are probably at high risk for suicide for other reasons. Certainly, the evidence is abundant that substance abuse, depression, and suicide are closely linked. Perhaps in a future edition of the DSM we'll see a Coffee Use Disorder diagnosis for people who drink 8+ cups a day.

The studies aren't definitive. We still can't say for sure that coffee-drinking *prevents* suicide. But it's starting to look as though it's at least *possible* that the cheapest, most effective, most widely available suicide-prevention drug in the world might well be none other than caffeine.

So don't skimp on the coffee. The evidence says it's associated, in dose-response fashion, with lowered rates of depression and (when drunk in moderation) reduced risk of suicide.

---

26 Kawachi *et al.* (1996), "A Prospective Study of Coffee Drinking and Suicide in Women," *Arch Intern Med.* 156:5, 521-525.
doi:10.1001/archinte.1996.00440050067008
27 Tanskanen *et al.* (2000), "Heavy coffee drinking and the risk of suicide," *European Journal of Epidemiology* 2000, Volume 16, Issue 9, pp 789-791

Anger Is Poison

Anger is one of the most toxic emotions you can live with, other than guilt (which, oddly enough, goes hand-in-hand with anger).

You need to go on an anger fast.

Just cut anger out of your life. If that sounds hard, try it for one day only, at first. Then work your way up to seven days a week.

People have been intuitively aware of the harmful connection between anger and health for centuries. Buddhism refers to it as one of the Three Poisons of the Mind (viz., greed, anger, and foolishness). Anger has received considerable attention in the medical community with regard to coronary heart disease (CHD). Early research seemed to show that "type A" behavior—characterized by hostility, intense ambition, competitive "drive," preoccupation with deadlines, and a sense of time urgency—was related to the development of heart disease, but the early findings were not supported by subsequent research. One possible reason for this is that some studies were prospective studies whereas others were retrospective case-control studies. This makes a difference, because retrospective studies are subject to recall bias caused by memory distortion, and thus cannot reliably detect an association between predictors and outcome variables.

In 2009, University College London researchers Yoichi Chida and Andrew Steptoe undertook a systematic review and meta-analysis of *prospective cohort studies* in order to better quantify the presumed causal association of anger and hostility with coronary heart disease. They looked at 25 studies of initially healthy populations and a further 19 studies of people already diagnosed with coronary heart disease (to see if anger changed cardiac outcomes in already-diagnosed patients). They found that anger and hostility were associated with increased CHD events in the healthy population studies; the increased risk was 19%. They found, also, that anger increased the risk of a bad outcome (by 24%) for patients with CHD.[28]

Anger and depression often go together. In a study of people who had recovered from a major depression with those who had never been depressed, the depressed-and-recovered (D/R) group significantly exceeded the never-depressed group in the degree to which they reported holding anger in and being afraid to express it. Also, D/R patients were more likely to endorse attitudes consistent with "silencing the self" theory, believing they must hide their feelings to preserve relationships. They were also more likely to have experienced an anger attack.[29]

There are three things you can do with anger: express it, hold it in, or let go of it. Each can be difficult. Holding it in is seldom a good strategy, for a lot of reasons (the main one being, the anger doesn't go away, but grows; and meanwhile, you feel a loss a self-esteem). Constructive expression of anger, on the other hand, is tricky, because it can go wrong; it can mean confrontation and needless damage to relationships. (There's an old saying: "Hurt people hurt people.") Some therapists recommend stomping on aluminum cans or buying a Wiffle Ball bat and using it to beat pillows or other objects. That may work for some people. I don't know any such people, personally.

Letting go of anger is the best option, but also the most difficult one. It may help to realize that anger often has three components:

28 Chida, Y. & Steptoe, A. (2009), "The Association of Anger and Hostility With Future Coronary Heart Disease : A Meta-Analytic Review of Prospective Evidence," *Journal of the American College of Cardiology*, 53:11, 17 March 2009, 936–946. Online: http://www.sciencedirect.com/science/article/pii/S0735109708041259 (retrieved 29 Jan. 2015).

29 Brody, C. et al. (1999), "Experiences of Anger in People Who Have Recovered from Depression and Never-Depressed People," *Journal of Nervous & Mental Disease* 187:7, 400-405.

resentment, hostility, and fear. Fear is future-facing, resentment is past-facing; hostility is in the present. All are toxic.

Letting go is a four-part process that I call face, feel, heal, and deal. The first step is to articulate the problem in words. Write down what it is that bothers you; it may be a long list of things. Name names. State your grievance(s) in detail. Admit that you have grievances (face them) and be clear about what they are.

The "feel" part is a matter of acknowledging the damaging effects these things have had on your state of mind. This is something you should consider doing in the presence of a therapist. Bring your list of grievances and go through them, telling how they make you feel. The important thing is to be heard. You can't hold resentments in; they have to be heard by *someone*. A wise person once said: "Resentments are like swallowing poison and expecting the other person to die." Bring resentments to the surface so they don't poison *you*.

The healing process begins when you go the next step and try to understand *your* role in each of the things that bothers you. Maybe you failed to speak up at key points in a stressful situation. Maybe you *undermined yourself* in various ways. Be honest about how you could have handled the situation differently. What *would* it have taken to make things come out differently? This is a very difficult step that requires honest self-appraisal. You can't duck *your* role in your own anger.

Finally, you have to *deal* with the present-day situation, the residue of toxic emotions. This is where a therapist trained in Cognitive Behavioral Therapy can help. CBT is not a cure-all, but it has valuable things to teach with regard to recognizing distortions of thought, ineffective modes of reasoning, and inappropriate (illogical, ineffective) responses to problems.

When you're ready—after you've worked your way through these steps—take your written list of grievances, the physical list of problems (you printed it out, right? or wrote it in a notebook?) and bury them out back. Literally. Go out in the back yard, dig a hole, and bury your hatreds. Or set them on fire and scatter the ashes. This physical ritual is an important symbolic way of telling yourself that you have, in fact, dealt with the problem and are ready to make a fresh beginning. It's optional, but recommended.

You will benefit from the help of a good therapist in dealing with anger. It's essential to be heard during this process. The people you're angry with may be dead or gone from your life; maybe your anger goes back to things that happened many years ago. Who's left to listen to you, besides yourself, your God, your therapist, your best friend, your dog? Choose one or more of the above, and *let yourself be heard.*

But don't undercut your success here by failing to take personal stock of *your* role in whatever led to the anger. *You* played a key role in whatever happened. You must acknowledge that fact, or healing can't happen.

Letting go of resentment often calls for forgiveness. You have to be able, on some level, to forgive those who hurt you. This is extremely hard, at first. It may be easier if you're a Christian and can commit yourself to obeying Jesus's invocation to love your enemies. Remember Matthew 5:44? "But I say unto you, Love your enemies, bless them that curse you, do good to them that hate you, and pray for them which spitefully use you, and persecute you." This is not Jesus giving *advice*; it's not a request. It's a direct order. It's Jesus *telling* you to love your enemies.

You don't have to be a Christian to benefit from this concept. It's actually a fairly deep concept, because once you act on it, you're liberated. You're set free. You've regained the moral high ground. You've put the other person in his or her place—in perspective—as a human being (a *flawed* one, but a human being nonetheless). Have you tried forgiveness as a strategy? If not, you should. Just as an experiment.

There was a time in my life when I felt tremendous anger over something that I felt put me in bondage, unfairly. I hated the person who "did this to me." My frustration over it nearly made me kill myself. I even toyed with the idea of killing the other person.

Relief didn't come until I realized, first of all, that (as Nathaniel Branden has said) *no one is coming*. (See the section of this book called "Claim Ownership," page 106.) The next great bit of progress came when I examined, critically, with brutal self-honesty, *my* role in creating my predicament. There was no doubt about the fact that I had handled the entire situation poorly, *to my own detriment*. Eventually, I began to experience a sense of detachment and objectivity that I hadn't experienced before; I found I could look at my situation and say, dispassionately, "Well, this is certainly shitty, isn't it?" as if viewing it from the outside, as a passive observer. It was almost humorous (in a perverse way). I went to therapy. I gave up alcohol. Over time, I began to acquire the strength, and the coping skills, to look at my situation non-judgmentally, logically, rationally, appropriately. And I realized that the person who hurt me was not a bad person, but *just a person*. People aren't all-good, nor all-bad. Even your worst enemy is *just a person*. The worst murderer in the world started life as a beautiful little baby that somebody loved. Even Hitler had a dog. (Of course, he poisoned it before killing himself.) The point is, villains aren't 100% villainous. They may not be good people, but they deserve a certain amount of empathy; they're victims of circumstance, too. Justice is important; I'm not saying it isn't. But be clear, justice and personal healing are two different things.

If you care about your own well-being, you'll let go of anger. You have to. Otherwise, you end up destroying *yourself*.

Laugh Inappropriately

I've always been fascinated by the term "inappropriate laughter." I tend to view laughter the way the French view champagne: always appropriate.

"Inappropriate humor" is another term that's foreign to me. It might as well be Sanskrit. I don't know how any humor can truly be called inappropriate. If that makes me sick, so be it.

It's hard to laugh when you're depressed (although frankly, I still find myself drawn to dark humor, even when I'm at my lowest). And I'm not suggesting there's anything funny about your situation, or that you should have someone tickle you just to get you to smile for a change.

But you should find a way to laugh *once in a while*.

And you don't need a reason. That's the beautiful part.

Zen monks sometimes engage in a "laughing meditation." Perhaps you've seen it on TV. They assemble in a room. At the stroke of a gong, all the monks begin to laugh—for no reason. They have to laugh whether they feel like it or not, because it's an exercise. But then something weird happens, because after a few minutes, the laughter becomes contagious, and soon everyone in the room is laughing genuinely, heartily, uncontrollably.

Have you tried the exercise? I know, exercise is repugnant. But that's because you're not doing it.

Remember the first time someone asked you to dance and you didn't feel like dancing? It turns out the only reason you didn't feel like dancing was because you weren't dancing. Once you agreed to dance, and got on the dance floor, it felt like it was the right thing to do after all.

American philosopher William James said: "We do not sing because we are happy, we are happy because we sing."

I was at a dorm party once, in college. We were dancing to some wild music. Suddenly, some genius decided to put on a mix-tape of Beatles songs, from the *Hard Day's Night* era. My initial reaction was: "What the *hell* are we listening to *this* old stuff for?" (Bear in mind, this was in 1971. The songs were less than ten years old, and already I considered them "oldies.") Within five minutes, even the most sober and stodgy wallflowers in the room were singing along with the Beatles at the top of their lungs, me included. It was an exercise in contagion, like the Zen laughing meditation. And I must say, it was therapeutic.

Listening to jokes is not a meaningful depression-fighting strategy, but laughing for no reason can be.

If you need to be in a room full of Zen monks to make it happen, go ahead and do that; but know that you can also tap into your inner monk.

Let's Not Talk about Willpower

A lot has been written about willpower (including whole books), much of it unhelpful, and I don't want to add to that morass with more meaningless chatter about the willpower we all know we want and don't have.

I don't think we should use the word *willpower* any more. It's outlived its uselessness.

Discussions of complex problems like substance abuse or depression shouldn't be framed in terms of willpower. I prefer to talk about *choices* and *decisions*. Basically, every time you make a decision, you've made a choice and have exercised willpower (to at least that small degree). In this sense, you exercise willpower *thousands* of times a day. Take what you're wearing, for example. You dressed yourself today, I'm guessing. That means you selected the top you're wearing; that was a choice. You selected the pants or skirt you're wearing; that was a choice. You selected the shoes you're wearing. Another choice.

If you get up off the couch to answer the phone, you've made a choice.

So don't tell me about not having willpower. We all have willpower. It's the ability to make, and act on, choices.

Where people get messed up is when they try to apply the concept of willpower to difficult things like changing a bad habit. Avoiding that next cigarette, if you're a smoker, involves willpower. I prefer to reframe the discussion, as I say, in terms of choices and decisions.

There are certain things in life we have no choice over: who our parents are, for example, or the fact that you have to eat (and go to the bathroom) every day whether you want to or not. You're probably thinking that much of your current mental distress, if you're depressed, comes from circumstances over which you have no choice. Fine. For sake of argument, let's lump that in with eating and going to the bathroom every day.

Here's the point I'm coming to: Even the things you think you have no choice over do, in fact, involve choices. You have to eat every day, but you get to exercise choice over what you'll put in your body. You can go through the drive-thru at McDonalds and get a burger and fries, or you can go to the store and pick up something perhaps a bit healthier to eat for lunch. It's your decision. One decision is the easy way out (McDonalds), the other takes a bit more effort (but doesn't really cost any more).

Every day, you have to cope with stress, including the stress of whatever it is that's making you depressed. Here, once again, you have choices. You can choose unhealthy coping mechanisms, like smoking or drinking or denial or pouting (the McDonalds of coping mechanisms), or you can go the extra mile and choose healthier coping mechanisms (metaphorically the equivalent of making your own lunch from fresh ingredients). You're probably choosing unhealthy coping mechanisms for the same reason people choose to eat at McDonalds: it's fast, easy, and familiar.

So here's the deal. Getting better—recovering from depression—involves effort. It doesn't have to involve a Herculean effort of the "quit smoking cold turkey" type. What *is* necessary is that you commit to the idea of making your own lunch, so to speak, rather than zipping through the drive-thru. The drive-thru is easy and familiar, but *it's not good for you if you do it every day.*

Start by making small choices that move you in a healthy direction —just like you make *thousands* of small choices every day, about everything you do, including the things you don't want to do but have to do anyway. That, to me, is the essence of willpower: being able to make (and give yourself credit for) *small* choices that, over time, start to get you pointed in the right direction.

You've got to stop babying yourself with the notion that you lack willpower. We *all* lack Willpower (with a capital 'W'). But we all make choices—tens of thousands of them, every day.

If you're taking your brain through the drive-thru every day, instead of trying new things, that's a choice. No one's forcing you to eat at McDonalds; no one's forcing you to use crummy coping mechanisms. Why not try something different once in a while?

I recognize that (as I said in the Introduction) some people are too depressed even to make an effort to get better. If you're in that place right now, no one can help you but you. No therapist, no book, no pill, no person, no fairy godmother, can *bring you* a magic cure. You have to want to get better *and* you have to be willing to move in that direction, under your own power. Some things, no one can do *for* you.

But the mere fact that you *chose* to read these words right now proves you have willpower—all the willpower you need to get started on the road to recovery.

Stop Fearing Problems

It's a mistake to go through life fearing problems. Society teaches us that problems are bad; comfort is good. We all look for the easy way out. But really, do all problems *have* to be bad? What if you were to celebrate your problems—yes, *celebrate* them—instead of fearing them?

"Every problem in your life," Richard Bach once said, "carries a gift inside it."

Dr. Andrew Weil goes so far as to suggest (in his book *Spontaneous Healing*) that we regard illness as a gift. Illness can be a powerful impetus for change. For this reason, Weil says: "Perhaps it is the only thing that can force some people to resolve their deepest conflicts. Successful patients often come to regard it as the greatest opportunity they ever had for personal growth and development—truly a gift. Seeing illness as a misfortune, especially one that is undeserved, may actually obstruct the healing system. Coming to see the illness as a gift that allows you to grow may unlock it."

It may sound radical to say so, but maybe sometimes it can be useful to change your perspective so that problems look more like unresolved opportunities—the "before" frame of a before/after picture in which the "after" picture is a happy one in which you're congratulating yourself on a job well done.

It's said that when people took their problems to legendary insurance magnate W. Clement Stone, he'd shout out: "You've got a problem? That's *great!*" (Amazingly, no one ever assassinated him.)

If you see all problems as curses, you'll live a cursed life. And that gets to be tiresome. Wouldn't you like to try a change?

You Are Not a Label

The list of "disorders" attributable to pathologies of mood is a long and ever-growing one that now includes anxiety, depression, suicide, homicide, rage and aggression, phobias, obsessions, compulsions, binge eating, anorexia, attention deficit, self-harm through cutting/burning, sexual deviance, sexual abstinence, addictions, various forms of withdrawal, combativeness, garrulousness, shyness, excitement, sloth, sociopathy, insomnia, hypersomnia, hedonism, anhedonia, egotism, self-hatred, etc. The *Diagnostic and Statistical Manual* (DSM), now in its fifth edition, lists hundreds of disorders. With each new edition, the list gets bigger.

An insurance-paid visit to a psychiatrist (to get pharmacological "treatment" for your symptoms) or to a licensed mental health counselor or psychologist (for talk therapy) brings with it the guarantee of having a DSM code, a diagnosis of mental disorder, put in your medical records. At first, you may feel an overwhelming sense of *relief* that at last, whatever it is that's been bothering you has been given a name. And of course, you're relieved to know that HIPAA laws, in the U.S., keep your clinicians from making the information public. But it's impossible not to also feel you've been labeled—because you have been. You now carry around with you a silent reminder that you're not *normal* any more; you're bipolar I, or have PTSD, or Borderline Personality Disorder, or Major Depressive Disorder, or whatever. And despite the understanding attitude of society towards victims of illness, you'll feel torn when it comes to discussing your condition with others, even people you trust, for fear of the stigma that still attaches to "mental illness."

It's vitally important, therefore, that you not attach undue significance to your "official diagnosis." Try not to let it eat away at your self-esteem. The DSM codes are a necessary artifact of the way health care is delivered these days. Insurance companies demand to see a code. There's no way to avoid it. Even if you go to a private therapist and pay for the visit yourself, it's likely your case file will contain a DSM diagnostic code of some kind.

Psychiatry has always been good at coming up with labels; that's what you do when you can't come up with bonafide cures—treatments that reliably work. Because there are no biological markers for mental disorders, collections of symptoms (grouped together under various disorders) are all we have. Mainstream medicine, prior to the modern era, operated this way for centuries, cataloging diseases by the quality of the patient's fever, for example, or the color of their phlegm.

Vocabulary-based medicine is a poor substitute for real medicine, but in the case of psychiatry it's all we have. The DSM is concerned mostly with symptoms (not even etiologies), placing psychiatry somewhere in the 1600s relative to the rest of medicine. Or maybe the late 1700s, since psychiatry is, after all, in the business of treating schizophrenia and depression with galvanic stimulation (electroshock), a "therapy" that has no known basis in science and whose only lasting effects are long-term cognitive deficits (see the Appendix on Electroshock Therapy later in this book).

If it makes you feel any better, just remember: You are not a collection of symptoms. You are not a DSM code. You are not a label.

My wife has schizophrenia. I never call her a schizophrenic, and if you meet someone with schizophrenia, I recommend you not use the noun (the label) *schizophrenic*. You can say someone has schizophrenia or has symptoms of psychosis. (Psychosis is a state or status, not a disease. Just like chest congestion is a state, not a disease per se; it may be associated with a cold, the flu, tuberculosis, or any number of things. Psychotic symptoms, likewise, can be associated with schizophrenia, dissociative disorders, severe depression, PTSD, a bad drug reaction, or any number of things.)

If you're depressed, you suffer from *symptoms of depression.* You're not a depressive, or a manic-depressive. You're not a label.

If you have mood swings, you suffer from bipolar symptoms.

If you're suffering symptoms of mania, you're not a *maniac.*

We need to get away from labels (nouns) and start using *adjectives* that talk about *symptoms,* because that's really all the DSM is concerned with.

Also remember, all mental "illness" is defined on a statistical basis, using the idea of *norms.* (Let us not forget, the DSM has "Statistical" in its title.) This idea has an important implication: namely, mental disorders occur *on a spectrum.* (Only if you're "outside the normal range," on this spectrum, are you considered "ill.") I've known hundreds of people with mental disorders. I've read *hundreds* of scientific papers in detail (and read the abstracts of probably 2,000 papers that were paywalled). One thing I'm utterly convinced of is that almost all mental disorders are *spectrum disorders.* Dysfunction occurs on a spectrum.

Example: We all talk to ourselves sometimes (which is a classical sign of schizophrenia) and many of us hear voices in our heads or have conversations with an imaginary friend (named God), etc. These are schizophrenia symptoms. You might ask yourself, if you're one of those people who frequently talks (out loud) to God, what makes *you* so different from the crazy "bag lady" who walks down the street muttering gibberish to no one in particular. The only thing that makes you different is that you have ready access to reality; you can return to reality any time you want and function within its rules. The bag lady can't. But you both exist on a spectrum. She's at one end of the "talking to yourself" spectrum and you're at some other end. See what I'm saying?

Maybe you believe in lucky numbers. The idea that a number has a particular *power* or *significance* beyond its prosaic numerical significance is irrational: such ideas are characteristic of schizophreniform mentation.

If you're a baseball fan and you wear your cap inside out during the 7th inning when your team is behind (a common practice), that's demented. It's arguably a symptom of illness! But you're not ill, because you have ready access to reality when you need it.

As a child, maybe you were careful to walk on the sidewalk a certain way. "Step on a crack, break your mother's back!" That has no basis in reality—it's schizophreniform thinking.

The point is, we all live on a spectrum. Depending where you fall on that spectrum, you either qualify for a DSM disorder or you don't.

The other thing I've noticed about mental "illness" (in quotes, because I don't believe there is a sound scientific basis for calling these things *illnesses* in the true medical sense) is that no two people's "illnesses" are the same. I've never met two schizophrenia sufferers whose pathology was the same. Each is uniquely different. One person may have religious hallucinations and talk to angels; another has no hallucinations but thinks every helicopter that flies overhead is the FBI checking on them. One person thinks orange sweaters are "danger," another thinks every black cat is Satan. One person is catatonic, another isn't.

The same goes for depression. Your depression may be *completely different* from my depression. Your problems and your coping styles will be different from my problems and my coping mechanisms Your particular pathology is not the same as anyone else's.

Our sense of *individuality* gets lost when we use labels. That's one of the horrible side effects of the current ridiculous trend toward "medicalization" of mental illness.

There's too much emphasis on labels, too little emphasis on suffering and what to do about it.

Reject labels. Get on with the serious business of dealing with suffering.

Claim Ownership

This is an advanced tip and you should realize up front that, even if you're ready to apply it (which you might not be, yet), it's likely to be disorienting and painful. But if you can absorb this lesson, this one will have a big payoff, potentially.

It's very simple.

Take ownership of your situation.

Be the responsible party—the person without whom none of your problems would exist—and claim ownership of your problems. Be the owner of record. *Be* the problem. Admit that you're where your problems start, and where they end.

Sounds awful, doesn't it?

After all, you wouldn't be in the situation you're in if it weren't for *those people* (whoever they are: your parents, your ex-, your boss, the bullies in your life) who traumatized you. You wouldn't be suffering if it weren't for the unjust external circumstances that brought you so much pain. *Everything* can't be your fault. Surely the people who visited trauma on you should get *some* of the credit.

Hey listen. Yes, those people were evil. Whoever bullied you, raped you, beat you, lied to you, tortured you, put you in hell—whoever those people are, their sins were sins; and if there's a God, He'll deal with them. But meanwhile, here you are, now, suffering. Whatever happened, happened. And it sucks. Terribly.

But from this day forward, what happens to you is *up to you*. It's not up to someone else to fix. It's your life. You have to own it now.

Seeing yourself as the *victim* of your problems deprives you of the power to solve them. As a result, you'll always look outside yourself for solutions. You'll look for external fixes: drugs, therapy, sympathy, articles, books, advice. But the things that need fixing aren't on the outside—and guess what? The "fix" isn't going to come in a cardboard box delivered by an Amazon drone. It's not going to fall out of the sky, into your lap.

Once you begin to see yourself as the sole owner of your problems, it's possible (then, and only then) for you to also be the *solution*.

This is a radical change of perspective for most people, because most people truly believe their problems were thrust on them by outside circumstances and other people. And it's true, external events can be cruel. But trauma is internal, not external.

It's a truism that trauma specialists know only too well: There is no such thing as a *traumatic event*, per se, because trauma is what you *experience*; the trauma is not the event itself. It's what happened inside *you*.

It's rare that you can fix something that happened to you by going back out into the world to right the wrong. I'm not saying you shouldn't seek justice if an injustice was done. What I'm saying is that justice and healing are two different things. If you were raped, the rapist should be put in jail, yes. Definitely. But putting the rapist in jail doesn't unrape you. Does that make sense?

Your current situation is what matters.

Own the situation so that it doesn't own you.

Psychologist Nathaniel Branden has an even more brutal way of putting it: "No one is coming."

No therapist is coming with the magic insight that's going to unlock the doors to Hell and set your spirit free. No book (including this one) is going to give you that special, priceless advice that's going to turn your life around. No Zen master is going to show you the key to enlightenment. No miracle pill, no miracle solution, is going to put things right, like magic.

There is no magic.

No one is coming.

That's really the bottom line.

The moment you can *accept* that no one is coming (which I'm sure you already know, anyway, somewhere deep in your heart)—the moment you can *embrace* that concept—it's a transformative moment, because it means *you* are the one with the ultimate power. No one *needs* to come.

The fact that no one is coming means you have nothing left to fear. (Think about that.)

It also means that when (not if) you get better, *you can take full credit.*

Man, how great is *that?*

Of course, if you *prefer* to remain a helpless victim, waiting for someone else, or some external event or thing, to change your life, you can do that—you can choose to remain a helpless bystander and hope for an eventual miracle from the outside. But you may be waiting a long time.

There was a period in my life, during my 10+ years of major depression, when I thought every problem I had was not of my making; I'd simply been the victim of various unfortunate circumstances (which were mostly someone else's fault, of course). And you know, honestly, a lot of my problems *were* caused by external events, some of them my fault, some not. A lot of it was situational. It doesn't matter. What matters is that I now own the consequences of those past events; I own the trauma. The trauma is my *reaction* to those events and their aftermath. That's something *I* own. No one else can claim it.

But be clear: Past events are in the past. You can't change them. So don't even try. Stop worrying about things you can't change! It's wasted energy.

Focus on what you *can* change. Mostly, that's *you.*

The good news is, you own you. You have the keys to the kingdom. No one else does.

"No one is coming" sounds like a message of despair, but it's not. Not really. It's a confirmation of what you already know. Embrace it and you'll be on solid ground—which is always a good place to start from.

Give of Yourself

In his autobiography, *They Call Me Coach*, John Wooden says: "You cannot live a perfect day without doing something for someone who will never be able to repay you." (John Bunyan said essentially the same thing.)

When researchers examined the Wisconsin Longitudinal Study, which surveyed 10,000 Wisconsin high school graduates from the class of 1957, they found that people who said, in their mid-30s, that helping others in their work was important were apt to report being more satisfied with their lives nearly three decades later. A followup study found, likewise, that those who help others are happier at work than those who don't prioritize helping others.[30] But this isn't about being happier *at work*. It's about being happier in life.

A substantial amount of evidence exists to show that altruism and subjective well-being are correlated. It's not *just* a correlation, though. It's causation. According to a 2012 study, "Evidence even suggests a causality mechanism after a number of studies showed that people who performed random acts of kindness for a period of time were happier than those in the control group."[31]

I can cite scientific papers until we're both blue in the face, but the

30 Moynihan, D., DeLeire, T., Enami, K. (2013), "A Life Worth Living: Evidence on the Relationship Between Prosocial Values and Happiness," *The American Review of Public Administration* July 4, 2013, doi: 10.1177/0275074013493657.

31 Calvo, R. *et al.* (2012), "Well-Being and Social Capital on Planet Earth: Cross-National Evidence from 142 Countries," *PLoS One*, doi: 10.1371/journal.pone.0042793. See also Lyubomirsky, S., Sheldon, K.M., Schkade, D. (2005) "Pursuing happiness: The architecture of sustainable change," *Review of General Psychology* 9: 111–131. doi: 10.1037/1089-2680.9.2.111

truth of the matter is easy to settle: Try your own experiment. Perform a random act of kindness every day for a week. Then see for yourself how you feel.

The research on this is so clear and obvious, you really shouldn't hesitate to accept it, so try it out. Do something for someone. Take the experiment even further: Try doing it *anonymously*, so there's no way the person can thank you.

Give an anonymous gift for a whole *community* of people. Example: Buy a book (maybe a copy of this one?) and donate it to a local library.

Or do one kind thing for a stranger. Just because.

You'll feel better instantly.

Tears for Fears

I was born male and have accepted that gender assignment with a genuine, abiding gratitude. I have seldom, if ever, regretted being born male—except for one thing, which I in fact regret bitterly, with a bitterness that borders on rage.

Like most little boys in this and many other cultures around the world, I was taught not to cry. From an early age, I was subjected to the "boys don't cry" cultural narrative, a monstrously cruel, abhorrent perversion of nature.

My entire adult life, I've been unable to cry, even under circumstances that demand it.

That's not 100% true any more. I *can* cry now (I've spent a lifetime regaining that precious skill), but only with extraordinary difficulty. I consider it a true handicap. I want my blue parking permit.

Seriously, crying is a tremendous tool to have. I realize its healing potential now. For years, I was deprived of experiencing it. I mourn for *that*, believe it or not.

As a man, you grow up trained to *tough it out, suck it up, man up,* etc., ad nauseam. You grow up thinking women who cry at the movies are addle-brained ninnies.

Guys? Guess what? *The joke's on us.*

Crying is priceless. It's cleansing. I can't begin to describe the benefits if you've never experienced them. (If you're a woman reading that last sentence, believe me when I tell you in all seriousness, there are, indeed, men who literally *know nothing* about crying; men who've never experienced the benefits, have no idea there *are* benefits to it.)

If you're a woman, imagine how crippling it would be if you could never cry. Imagine, if you can, losing a loved one *and not being able to cry*. Think of the torture to the soul that would cause. Think how messed up you'd be, how incapable you'd be of bringing grief to the surface, how emotionally stunted you'd feel. Think what that would do to you.

That's where I lived for decades. That's how most men live, all the time.

My parents died. I didn't cry until years later.

Things happened to me in childhood that I didn't cry about until *forty years later.*

How do you regain the ability to cry? There's no single foolproof method. It differs for each person. If you're a man reading this, and you haven't cried in years (or decades, maybe), you're missing out. You need to learn this skill. I imagine you can learn it in a good acting class (although many actors do admit crying on demand is one of the harder skills to acquire). I've had to invent my own ad hoc methods.

I still can't cry on demand, when I need to. I have to trick myself into it. I can tell you some of the tricks that work for me, even though they may not work for you. They're laborious. They involve playing movies and songs. My hope is that in a few more years, I'll have learned to do without the tricks. Like a disciplined actor, I'll be able to reach into that special place where the right emotions live, and go straight to the wet-works, as needed. I'm not there yet. Not even close.

You know the movie *Awakenings*? Robin Williams plays the New York physician who gave L-dopa to institutionalized catatonia patients in 1969—patients left profoundly disabled by the 1918 epidemic of encephalitis lethargica. For the first time in 50 years, the patients regain the ability to move, walk, speak. Eventually, the drug slowly loses its effect and the patients go back to their pathetic catatonia. But the Robin Williams character learns something about hope, in a way he couldn't have otherwise.

That movie has brought me to tears more than once. It did so long before Robin Williams died. Now it's even sadder, of course. Plus I'm married to someone who, had she been born 75 years earlier, would have been in an institution of the kind shown in that movie; my wife has schizophrenia. And as I watch her slide into and out of psychosis (as the drugs work, then fade, then have to be replaced with other drugs that work, then fade) my heart slowly breaks, then heals. Breaks, then heals.

The *Awakenings* story arc is similar to that of another favorite "crying tool" of mine, the novel *Flowers for Algernon* by Daniel Keyes. In it, a profoundly retarded man, Charlie Gordon, submits to an experimental surgery that gives him intelligence—not just *normal* intelligence, but monumental intelligence. It changes his entire life, of course, in expected and unexpected ways. Meanwhile, the laboratory mouse, named Algernon, who had the surgery first, "proving" its safety and effectiveness, unexpectedly begins to deteriorate (and dies). Charlie, in turn, also begins to regress, slowly at first, then ever-faster.

The 1968 movie *Charly* (based on the Keyes book) won an Oscar for Cliff Robertson (Best Actor), but with all due respect to Robertson, the book is far more moving than the film.

Flowers for Algernon is written in an epistolary form (in first person, by the Charlie Gordon character, who has an IQ of 68), so the writing initially contains many misspellings ("progris riport 1 martch 3"—Charlie calls the Rorschach test a "raw shok test," etc.), but of course, by the middle of the book, the Charlie character is writing like an intellectual giant. Then he regresses.

I've made a lot of progress with *Flowers for Algernon*. It used to take me 30 or 40 pages of reading to start to tear up. Now I get misty-eyed after looking at the first two or three pages of that book. Soon I should just be able to think of the book in my mind and feel the tears starting to come. I lack the emotional availability to do that right now, though. But I'm getting there.

Why does that book provoke tears in me? I don't know. I'm not sure I *need* to know, right now. I'm just glad it works.

Call me sappy, but the climactic scene of *Good Will Hunting* also "does it" for me. You know the scene where Robin Williams (the psychologist character) says, over and over again, as Will looks at photographs of the physical abuse inflicted on him as a child, "It's not your fault"? That. That works for me. I know someone who was abused as a child. I know what that does to a person. I also know that some things are far worse than mere *physical* abuse. Your body gets over physical abuse (assuming you survive it, of course). Your mind? That's another story.

The right music can move me to tears, under the right circumstances. Strap me to a chair and make me listen to a couple of Karla Bonoff albums and I'll crack, guaranteed. (Get the mop.)

I haven't tried this yet, but I think maybe a good technique for me, to take my emotional availability (in terms of crying) to the next level, might be to find a song that's deeply affecting *and* ties in, thematically, with the book *Flowers for Algernon*; then practice reading the first few pages of the Keyes book *with that song playing*. I have near-photographic memory for music (if that metaphor even makes sense); I can remember a recording in exquisite detail, and "play it back" in my head any time I want. Who knows if maybe, with practice, I'll get to the point where I can "play back" the *Algernon* song (whatever that turns out to be) in my head and bring forth the emotional wherewithal to cry, *on demand*. That would be an achievement.

If you're one of those people who can cry easily, count your blessings. You don't know how good you have it.

Learn from the Dying

In 2013, Bronnie Ware—a nurse in a palliative care unit—conducted an interesting survey. She decided to poll her terminally ill patients, in their last days, in hopes of uncovering their regrets so others could learn from them.

You've probably seen the short version (five items) of this list before, since it's made the rounds on the Internet quite a few times. But maybe you've never seen the full list of ten items. Here they are—the top ten regrets of the dying:

1. I never pursued my dreams and aspirations.
2. I worked too much and never made time for my family.
3. I should have made more time for my friends.
4. I should have said "I love you" a lot more.
5. I should have spoken my mind instead of holding back and resenting things.
6. I should have been the bigger person and resolved my problems.
7. I wish I had children.
8. I should have saved more money for my retirement.
9. I wish I'd had the courage to live truthfully.
10. Happiness is a choice; I wish I knew that earlier.

I leave it to you to analyze and digest this list, and take from it what you will. Personally, I agree with all of the items except the final item, which I only partly agree with. For many severely depressed people, happiness is not *simply* a matter of choice. If it were, they'd choose it.

The claim that happiness is a choice is simplistic and puts blame on the depressed person. It basically says that if you aren't happy, it's because *you chose unhappiness*. I can't think of a less helpful thing to tell someone who's suicidal than "happiness is a choice," even though I understand the good intention behind the message.

"Happiness is a choice" overlooks situational catastrophes (the kind people definitely do *not* choose) that are known to lead to depression, such as cancer, bankruptcy, divorce, prison time, death of a loved one, etc. Do you dare go up to someone whose child just died of leukemia and say: *Happiness is a choice?* Seriously?

The goal of therapy is to *get* to a point where happiness is, in fact, a choice. Some people never get there. And I feel sad for those people. The *last* thing I'm going to do to a person like that is kick dirt in their face by saying "Happiness is a choice."

Nevertheless, I understand the motivation behind this corny, trite, creepy, unhelpful saying, I think, which is: There are many roads to *contentment* or *subjective well-being* (which are more useful terms than "happiness"), and we have more control over the choice of road than we often think we do. This is a much more accurate, appropriate, nuanced, helpful way of saying the same thing, in my opinion.

Or maybe we can agree to say: Happiness is a choice *eventually*. Meaning: It's possible you'll get to a point, eventually, in your journey of self-discovery, where you'll realize that subjective well-being is not something "out there," over the horizon, beyond the yellow-brick road; it's something that's *right here, right now*. It's something you work to achieve; but it *is* achievable. The starting point is honesty and self-acceptance (which includes acceptance of pain and confusion, unfortunately). The road to well-being is long and twisted. There are switchbacks, detours, delays, wrong turns, road kill. It's not a simple straight-line point-A-to-point-B journey. If it were, everyone would be at the finish line already, drinking champagne.

Nevertheless, remember the words of the dying. There's no reason *you* should have to make any of the statements on that list of ten items, now that you know, in advance, what needs to be done.

Appendices

120

Mind over Matter

The recent fascination with biological theories of mental illness has caused many scientists (and others) to overlook, forget, or downplay a substantial medical literature on the powers of the *mind*, as opposed to the brain. Some of the earlier accounts of mind feats (going back to Freud's time) are worth revisiting, though, because they remind us that the mind is more powerful than we sometimes imagine.

Mere suggestion (whether done under hypnosis or not) is, by itself, a powerful thing. A century ago, one of few therapies available for hemophiliacs was hypnotic suggestion to control bleeding. The best-known case is that of the Russian monk Rasputin, who was said to have been able to stop the bleeding of the Czar's hemophiliac son by power of suggestion. McCord (1968)[32] reports the case of a patient whose frequent nosebleeds responded "poorly" to conventional treatment but stopped, at least up to a three-month followup point, after a single hypnotic suggestion ("given ... in a definite and purposeful manner"). Clawson and Swade (1975)[33] reported immediately halting the bleeding of a severe laceration, by suggestion. There are reports of gastrointestinal bleeding (of ulcers) having been stopped this way as well. Barber (1984)[34] describes the use of hypnotic

---

32 McCord, H. (1968), "Hypnotic control of nosebleed," *American Journal of Clinical Hypnosis*, 10:3, 219.

33 Clawson, T.A. & Swade, R.H. (1975), "The hypnotic control of blood flow and pain: the cure of warts and the potential for the use of hypnosis in the treatment of cancer," *American Journal of Clinical Hypnosis* 17:3, 160-9.

34 Barber, Theodore X. (1984), " Changing "unchangeable" bodily processes by (hypnotic) suggestions: A new look at hypnosis, cognitions, imagining, and the mind–body problem," *Advances in Mind-Body Medicine* 1:2, 7-40.

suggestion to control bleeding in dental surgery, particularly in hemophiliacs.

The reports of control over bleeding using hypnotic suggestion may sound improbable, but many cases have been documented (*well documented, in reputable journals*) of increases or decreases in heart rate, blood flow, and/or body temperature (in specific parts of the body) in yogis and shamans who have shown an unusual ability to control their bodies in meditative trances.

James Esdaile (1808–1859) conducted hundreds of surgeries using "mesmerism," which was the only anesthetic (other than alcohol) available for most of his career, chloroform not becoming available until 1850. He was a reluctant mesmerist who seized on the technique (without prior training, having only heard of it second-hand) out of desperation. Some of the surgeries Esdaile performed would now be considered unthinkable without anesthesia, including many testicular operations, amputations, and (in one case) removal of a facial tumor that compromised the orbit of one of the patient's eyes.

In a fairly recent (2003) randomized, controlled study of 18 women who underwent reductive mammoplasty, surgical wounds healed faster (by blinded assessment) in a group given hypnotic suggestion than in two control groups.[35]

Many cases have been reported of burns healing faster in hypnotic-suggestion groups than in other groups. In one case[36], the patients served as their own controls: Each had suffered burns on both sides of the body (usually the hands), but the hypnotic suggestion was directed at one side only, chosen randomly. Four of five patients showed "clearly accelerated healing on the treated side," as assessed by a physician unaware of which side had been "treated." (The fifth patient had rapid healing on both sides, perhaps because he wanted to heal

35 Ginandes C., Brooks P., Sando W., Jones C., Aker J. (2003), "Can medical hypnosis accelerate post-surgical wound healing? Results of a clinical trial," *American Journal of Clinical Hypnosis*. 45:4,:333-51.

36 Moore L.E., Kaplan J.Z.(1983) "Hypnotically accelerated burn wound healing," *American Journal of Clinical Hypnosis* 26:1,16-9.

quickly on *both* sides rather than be limited by the experimental protocol.)

H.F. Dunbar, in *Emotions and Bodily Changes*, 4th Ed. (Columbia University Press, 1954), describes the case of a physician who had suffered a severe x-ray burn, effects of which persisted for 14 years, with painful swelling and scars so severe that another physician suggested amputation. After four weeks of hypnotic treatment, the symptoms were improved; and a year later, healing was complete.

The literature contains reports of various serious skin conditions responding to hypnotherapy. Barber (see earlier footnote) refers to ten cases of ichthyosiform eryhtrodermia, or "fish-skin disease," that responded, in one degree or another, to hypnotic suggestion. In one case[37], the patient was a teenage boy whose entire body was affected. The physician began with treatment of just the left arm. Improvement was immediate: "Five days later, the horny layer softened, became friable, and fell off. The skin underneath became pink and soft within a few days." At the end of 10 days, "the arm was completely clear from the shoulder to the wrist." Treatment proceeded to the other arm, then the legs and trunk. Improvements ranged from 50% to 95% for different parts of the body. After four years, "not only has there been no relapse, but his skin has continued to improve . . . without further treatment of any kind, hypnotic or otherwise."

Mullins, Murray, and Shapiro (1955) reported on a case of pachyonychia congenita, a condition similar to ichthyosis, which responded to hypnotherapy.[38] Treatment began with just the left hand; "within three days, there was noticeable softening of the keratotic material on the left hand." Treatment continued, successfully, and the authors published photos of the soles of the patient's feet. When the patient had been admitted to the hospital, his condition was so painful,

---

37 Mason, A.A. (1952), "Case of Congenital Ichthyosiform Erythrodermia of Brocq treated by Hypnosis," *Br Med J*. Aug 23, 1952; 2(4781): 422–423.

38 Mullins, J.F., Murray, N., Shapiro, E.M. (1955) "Pachyonychia congenita; a review and new approach to treatment," *AMA Arch Dermatol* 71: 264–268.

he couldn't walk (and had to use a wheelchair). By the thirteenth day of treatment, the patient "stood on his feet without pain for the first time in his life that he could remember." By the seventeenth day, he was walking the halls.

The medical literature is filled with examples of the spontaneous disappearance of warts as a result of suggestion. In the 1920s, a German physician named Bloch developed an elaborate procedure in which blindfolded patients had their warts exposed to "x-rays" from a noisy machine that was not, in fact, an x-ray machine. (It did nothing but make noise.) Bloch painted the patients' warts with a harmless dye and sent them home with a warning not to touch their warts nor wash off the "medicine" until the warts were gone. Of 179 patients who were followed up, 78.5% were cured of their warts. The warts disappeared in weeks, even though many patients had had them for years, and all had tried other treatments without success.

Reports of hypnotic cures for warts are numerous and continue to appear in the literature. To counter the idea that these "cures" are simply resulting from the natural disappearance of warts over time, some experimenters have tried directing treatment to one or the other hand, in people who have warts on both hands. Many successes have been reported. In one case,[39] when treatment was begun, the intention was to remove all warts on both hands, but when the patient's warts began to shrink, the patient was given the suggestion that one particular wart be allowed to remain, as a kind of control; and after ten months, that was, in fact, the only wart that remained.

All of the proposed explanations for the curing of warts by suggestion are variations on the idea that blood flow to the warts has been affected ("vasomotor effects emotionally induced," in the words of one researcher). Such an explanation certainly accords well with the idea that bleeding can be reduced, in hemophilia, by suggestion; and it agrees with what we know about yogis who can control heart rate,

---

39 See, for example, Dreaper, R. (1978) "Recalcitrant warts on the hand cured by hypnosis," *The Practitioner*, 22, 305-310.

hand temperature, basal body temperature, etc., through mindfulness techniques. If we accept the idea that "mindfulness techniques" and suggestion can influence blood flow, it becomes possible to understand how a great variety of skin conditions can be influenced by hypnotic suggestion.

But maybe there are other mechanisms to consider, as well.

In 1975, Ader and Cohen showed, in a very famous experiment involving rats, that the immune system is modulated by the brain.[40] First, all rats were exposed to a powerful immunosuppressive drug (cyclophosphamide). Half were given the drug concurrently with saccharine, which has no immunosuppressive effects whatsoever. Over a period of two months, some animals continued to get saccharine every two days; others didn't. The ones continuously presented with saccharine were later found to be immunosuppressed (relative to the control animals) when challenged with an antigen (sheep's blood). Since saccharine, by itself, is not immunosuppressive, the experiment demonstrated that the animals "learned" to become immunosuppressed by saccharine. This study triggered a wave of subsequent experimentation in psychoimmunology, creating a vast literature showing that the brain, and learned behaviors, can influence immune system activity, cortisol levels, and much else.

Against this backdrop, we have studies like the one by Everson *et al.* (1996) that showed a definite link between hopelessness (which is arguably a learned response) and mortality in a study group of 2,428 patients. Said the researchers:

> We examined the relationship among low,
> moderate, and high levels of hopelessness, all-
> cause and cause-specific mortality, and incidence
> of myocardial infarction (MI) and cancer in a

---

40 Ader R., Cohen N. (1975), "Behaviorally conditioned immunosuppression," *Psychosom Med.* 1975 Jul-Aug;37(4):333-40. Available online at http://www.pnei-it.com/1/upload/conditioned_induced_immunosuppression_1975.pdf (retrieved 28 Jan. 2015).

population-based sample of middle-aged men. Participants were 2428 men, ages 42 to 60, from the Kuopio Ischemic Heart Disease study, an ongoing longitudinal study of unestablished psychosocial risk factors for ischemic heart disease and other outcomes. In 6 years of follow-up, 174 deaths (87 cardiovascular and 87 noncardiovascular, including 40 cancer deaths and 29 deaths due to violence or injury), 73 incident cancer cases, and 95 incident MI had occurred. Men were rated low, moderate, or high in hopelessness if they scored in the lower, middle, or upper one-third of scores on a 2-item hopelessness scale. Age-adjusted Cox proportional hazards models identified a dose-response relationship such that moderately and highly hopeless men were at significantly increased risk of all-cause and cause-specific mortality relative to men with low hopelessness scores. Indeed, highly hopeless men were at more than three-fold increased risk of death from violence or injury compared with the reference group. These relationships were maintained after adjusting for biological, socioeconomic, or behavioral risk factors, perceived health, depression, prevalent disease, or social support. High hopelessness also predicted incident MI, and moderate hopelessness was associated with incident cancer. Our findings indicate that hopelessness is a strong predictor of adverse health outcomes, independent of depression and traditional risk factors.[41]

This is by no means the only study of its kind; others can be found on Google Scholar or by reviewing pp. 123-124 of Kelly & Kelly, *Irreducible Mind* (Rowman & Littlefield Publishers, 2007).

Studies of conjugal bereavement show over and over again that the risk of mortality increases in bereaved spouses during the first two years after a loss, and particularly in men within six months.[42] One

---

41 Everson *et al.* (1996), "Hopelessness and risk of mortality and incidence of myocardial infarction and cancer," *Psychosom Med.* 1996 Mar-Apr;58(2):113-21.

42 See, for example, Helsing, K.J. & Szklo, M. (1981), "Mortality after bereavement," *Am. J. Epidemiol.* 114 (1): 41-52. See also Kaprio J., Koskenvuo

study measured lymphocyte function in 26 bereaved spouses two weeks and six weeks after their partners' deaths. The study showed depressed T-cell function, demonstrating a connection between bereavement and immune function.[43] These findings were replicated and extended by Schleifer *et al.* in 1983.[44]

We also have many studies associating stress with sudden death. A systematic study of 26 men who died suddenly and unexpectedly found that depression and/or an event that triggered acute anger preceded death.[45] In another study, of 100 men under age 70 who died suddenly, the vast majority had been found to have been under unusual stress within 30 minutes, 24 hours, or six months preceding death.[46] The researchers noted:

> The deaths of 100 men due to coronary artery disease which occurred so suddenly and unexpectedly as to merit a coroner's necropsy have been studied, with special reference to the exact circumstances of their occurrence. The most significant relationship of sudden death was with acute psychological stress. Moderate physical activity, the time of day, the day of the week, and a recent meal, especially if accompanied by alcohol, were also significantly related. Very strenuous exercise, the season of the year, the environmental temperature or recent change

M., & Rita H. (1987), "Mortality after bereavement: a prospective study of 95,647 widowed persons," *American Journal of Public Health* March 1987: Vol. 77, No. 3, pp. 283-287. The latter study looked at 95,647 widowed persons and found substantially increased mortality in both men and women, especially with regard to ischemic heart events.

43 Bartrop *et al.* (1977), "Depressed lymphocyte function after bereavement," *Lancet* 309:8016, 834–836.

44 Schleifer et al. (1983), "Suppression of lymphocyte stimulation following bereavement.," *JAMA.* 1983 Jul 15;250(3):374-7.

45 Greene, W.A., Goldstein S., Moss, A.J. (1972), "Psychosocial Aspects of Sudden Death: A Preliminary Report," *JAMA Internal Medicine* 129(5):725-731.

46 Myers A. & Dewar H.A. (1975), "Circumstances attending 100 sudden deaths from coronary artery disease with coroner's necropsies," *Br Heart J.* 1975 Nov;37(11):1133-43.

> of it, and chronic psychological stress were
> not so related. Neither were the actual
> smoking of a cigarette nor the composition of
> the meal immediately preceding death.

Obviously, it's not possible to state definitively, based on these sorts of reports, that stress can *cause* death, but the results are nonetheless quite suggestive. Ignore them at your own risk.

All of these studies (on hypnotic suggestion, psychoimmunology, stress, etc.) suggest that the powers of the mind are far-reaching, probably underestimated, and not well understood. The power of suggestion (hypnotic or otherwise), in particular, is considerable, and probably goes a long way toward explaining the placebo effect, which is robust across a vast range of studies involving a huge number of conditions (including diabetes, stroke, and breast cancer, as well as mental disorders).[47] Placebo effects are, of course, physiologically as real as real can be and shouldn't be discounted or underestimated.

The bottom line is that the mind can be harnessed to achieve powerful healing effects. Latent within each of us is an incredible reservoir of healing power capable of affecting blood flow to individual parts of the body, influencing the immune system, and modulating physical and mental health. If we can tap into this latent power, we can accelerate our recovery from serious mental and physical ailments. But we have to start by believing in the power of the mind and applying mindfulness techniques that can move us in a direction of health and wellbeing.

You may scoff at the idea that "mere suggestion" can cause a wart to disappear from your body, or reduce bleeding, or cause a skin condition to get better, or whatever. But have you ever really *tried* it? Can you honestly say you've *tried* applying suggestion ("auto-hypnosis," if you will; mindfulness) to the amelioration of warts, skin

---

47 See Leucht et al. (2012), "Putting the efficacy of psychiatric and general medicine medication into perspective: review of meta-analyses," *BJPysch* 200:97-106. Table I shows placebo response rates for a variety of non-psychiatric conditions, including diabetes, breast cancer, stroke, and other ailments.

problems, back pain, weight gain, mood problems? Have you *done the experiment?* If not, how can you say "mind over matter" doesn't work? Telling yourself these things *can't* work is, in a sense, a form of suggestion (that works). When you think something *won't* work, quite often it doesn't. Why not try the opposite? Try auto-suggestion. Try mindfulness. Try willing a wart to go away. Try willing back ache away. Try whatever you think might be beneficial, no matter how ridiculous it may seem, on the surface. The worst that can happen is nothing changes. The best that can happen is *everything* changes.

Your mind has the power to make remarkable things happen. Use that power to your advantage.

Is Mental Illness Biological?

Unfortunately, biological psychiatry, which assumes (incorrectly, in my opinion) that every mental disorder has a genetic and/or physiological and/or anatomical explanation, puts patients in an essentially powerless, hopeless position. The whole "illness" model, which began with alcoholism and is now applied to every disorder in the *Diagnostic and Statistical Manual of Mental Disorders* (the so-called DSM), basically relegates people to victim status. An alcoholic is no longer a person who made bad lifestyle choices (and can change them and get well again), but someone who is under the grip of a lifelong illness, and therefore can't help himself (and will never be "cured," according to Alcoholics Anonymous; the best he can hope for is to live "one day at a time"). What's even worse is that the biological model suggests mental problems may be, to some extent, genetic. That's a horrible curse, because it means you'll never be well unless you can rewire your DNA! At best, you'll have to take drugs the rest of your life, like "insulin for diabetes."

These conceptions of mental illness are tremendously damaging. They remove the possibility of proactive change and personal transformation from the healing equation (because after all, the sufferer is merely the victim of bad DNA and/or malfunctioning neurons and/or a mysterious "chemical imbalance"). In point of fact, there is no credible scientific evidence for a biological basis for any mental illness, since there's no blood test, no urine test, no fecal test, no MRI test, nor any other test that can definitively establish a person's "illness" status with respect to depression, schizophrenia, etc. (And I might add, scientists have not identified "alcoholism genes," despite many claims to the contrary.)

I review the scientific evidence, and refute the twin studies and other "heritability" claims, in my book *Of Two Minds*, so I won't recap that info here, except to say what many people inside and outside psychiatry have already said, which is that the biological model of mental illness is *not* well supported by evidence; it is speculative, at best. And a variety of studies have shown that the biological model, while it does reduce self-blame, also reduces optimism about recovery prospects.[48]

But there's another way to look at mental illness, which is that it's not traceable to hardware-level defects in DNA and/or enzymes, but rather, a software problem—a problem with the operating system, if you will: the mind. Under this model, there's no requirement for a "just so" molecular-genetic explanation of things. There's no need for a depression gene, a schizophrenia gene, or an alcoholism gene. The basic biological requirement for any of these ailments is simply to have a nervous system.

When you think about it, it makes sense. Do you remember a time when you weren't depressed, or didn't have alcoholism (or schizophrenia, or whatever)? Well, guess what? You had the same genes then that you have now. You have mostly the same neurons in your brain then that you have at this moment. What's changed? The software. The algorithms. The logic.

That means there's hope for recovery. Why? Because while you can't change your DNA, you *can* make upgrades to the operating system. You can patch the software. You can fix faulty logic.

---

48 See, for example, Mehta, S. & Farina, A. (1997), "Is Being "Sick" Really Better? Effect of the Disease View of Mental Disorder on Stigma," *Journal of Social and Clinical Psychology* Vol. 16, No. 4, pp. 405-419. Also see Phelan, J.C., Yang L., Cruz-Rojas, R. (2006), "Effects of Attributing Serious Mental Illnesses to Genetic Causes on Orientations to Treatment," Psychiatry Online Volume 57 Issue 3, March 2006, pp. 382-387. Available at http://psychiatryonline.org/doi/full/10.1176/appi.ps.57.3.382 (retrieved 28 Jan. 2015).

The biological model can't explain hope, faith, consciousness, the unconscious mind, curiosity, wonder, imagination, dreams, or personality. These things (which psychologists of Freud's day spent a lot of time studying) are not merely the sum of your neurotransmitters; hence, neuroscientists refuse to acknowledge their importance, much less study them. And yet, these things may be the key to understanding how the mind operates, and how the dysfunctional mind may be made whole again.

Things like hope and expectation play a huge role in the placebo effect, and we've seen (in the Appendix preceding this one) how profoundly important these little-understood powers of *mind* can be. The mind has incredible healing power.

The illness model is only that—a model. We rely on it as a convenience, because mental disorders have many of the superficial features of true illness: disability, accompanied by symptoms, that runs a course and (often) disappears after a period of convalescence. These features do not automatically prove that mental disorders are true biological illnesses, however, and it's a mistake to confuse mental illness with true biological illness. A true illness has biological markers: tissue abnormalities, physiological disturbances that can be measured, and in the case of true disease, communicability. Mental disorders have none of that. (When a mental disorder, such as Huntington's disease, acquires a valid molecular-genetic cause, it disappears from the DSM and becomes a bonafide neurological disease.) Any honest medical professional will admit that we *don't know* how mental illnesses work, on a molecular level.

We also don't know that these conditions are genetic, despite claims of "heritability." Imagine how foolish it would be if, because a Christian Scientist family named Smith refused vaccines for its children, and as a result every generation of Smith children got measles, therefore scientists jump to the conclusion that measles is "genetic," and a search begins for a "measles predisposition gene" in the Smith family. Or what if the Smith family has a long history of child abuse? We know that child abuse tends to be intergenerational: victims of child abuse often grow up to be abusers themselves. Are we now to look for a "child abuse gene"?

This kind of logic is absurd, and yet it's the logic followed by researchers who insist that because alcoholism, schizophrenia, depression, and many others disorders listed in the DSM "run in families," therefore there must be a genetic explanation.

With measles, we know the agent of transmission is a virus. Genes matter very little. The basic biological requirement for getting measles is to have a body with blood, tissues, nerves, mucous membranes, etc. Normal, everyday human-body genes are "measles susceptibility genes."

With alcoholism and other "mental illnesses," the biological prerequisite is to have a nervous system: genes for neurons, etc. The maladaptive patterns of behavior associated with substance abuse are acquired. They represent "thought viruses." They can infect any mind. In some cases they can be passed on, from generation to generation. There's no reason to believe a genetic explanation is necessary, and (in fact) to *bring in* genetic explanations is to violate the scientific principle of parsimony (known to non-scientists as Occam's Razor). Good scientific practice is to reject superfluous "just so" arguments. In science, the most minimal explanation wins, until there is *reason* to complicate the hypothesis with extra explanations.

Having said all this, we nevertheless should remain *open* to the possibility that someday genetic correlates of mental illness may be found. (They haven't yet been.) Current techniques have failed to find convincing evidence of genetic explanations for mental illness. Future techniques may, however, uncover new information. We're not there yet, though. It's premature to *assume* that mental illness is in any way genetic.

The genome-wide association studies (GWAS) that have looked for genes for alcoholism, depression, schizophrenia, etc. have found *some* SNPs (single nucleotide polymorphisms; common mutations, essentially) that are associated with these conditions, but the association is weak, because the amount of heritability that can be accounted for by the genetic variations found thus far is extraordinarily small. Even traits that we "know" are genetic, such as body height (estimated to be 80% to 90% genetic), are not well explained by GWAS research. Over 180 genetic features found via GWAS are thought to play a role in determining height, but the 180 features, put together, account for only 10% of the heritability of height.[49] This suggests GWAS is not the right tool to determine heritability. GWAS is based on partial genomic sequencing. Large numbers of SNPs (which you can think of as discrete point-samples) are compared against databases of common SNPs to determine association patterns. But the databases contain SNPs that are *common*, not fatal or seriously deleterious. Such SNPs represent neutral mutations without much phenotypic significance. (Phenotype is a fancy word for the physical manifestation of a gene; the trait it produces.) Therefore it is not surprising that the markers uncovered in GWAS are not capable of explaining heritability. They're neutral mutations. The positive associations that show up are probably mostly statistical flukes to begin with. Any time you look at half a million SNPs, some are bound to look like "positive markers" for disease, by sheer odds. But when the markers fail to predict heritability, it shows that they're spurious, or at least of miniscule importance.

What will it take, then, to resolve the genetic debate once and for all? It will take deep sequencing (not point sampling) of complete human genomes. But when that happens, it will create statistical analysis problems of truly prodigious proportions, because we'll be dealing with *billions* (not millions) of data points per genome—and we'll need to analyze *thousands* of genomes. To do the necessary

---

49 Allen, H.L., *et al.* (2010), "Hundreds of variants clustered in genomic loci and biological pathways affect human height," *Nature* 467, 832–838, online at http://www.nature.com/nature/journal/v467/n7317/abs/nature09410.html (retrieved 1 Jan. 2015).

statistical analyses, *truly massive* networks of computers (Amazon cloud, Google cloud, etc.) will need to be harnessed. It's by no means assured that we have the necessary computer power; new algorithms will probably need to be invented. All of this will eventually come to pass (perhaps in the next ten years), but it will be a formidable undertaking. And we're not there yet. We're *not even close* to being able to assign a definite genetic cause to depression, schizophrenia, etc.

Meanwhile, we do know that the logical conundrums of mental illness can (sometimes) be treated with talk therapy, and that hope and agency and the capacity for personal transformation play pivotal roles in recovery from mental illness. Instead of downplaying the importance of those factors (which we do when we focus myopically on biological correlates that can't be proven to exist), we should be exploiting the mind's superlative built-in healing powers, which we *know* exist. We know that the mind is capable of incredible, marvelous, unbelievably powerful feats. Let's focus on that for a change.

Electroconvulsive Therapy

In the last 50 years, there has been a prominent global movement toward *evidence-based medicine*, which has been defined as "the conscientious, explicit, and judicious use of current best evidence in making decisions about the care of patients" (Sackett *et al.* 1996)[50]. This well-established approach values the use of robust experimental protocols involving placebo control arms, random assignment of patients to control and treatment arms, double-blind techniques, predefined outcome measures, and intent-to-treat analysis, among other considerations.

Electroconvulsive therapy (ECT) has been an accepted treatment for schizophrenia and refractory depression for over 50 years, and it is widely promoted as a highly effective technique. Nevertheless, the vast majority of studies conducted on ECT have failed to include placebo (sham ECT) groups. Most of the studies that claim a high response rate for ECT patients lack a control arm and thus do not conform to modern standards of evidence-based medicine.

Until the 1950s, when general anesthesia was introduced for ECT, it was not possible to include a control arm in ECT studies, since there is no way to trick a fully-awake patient into thinking he's been shocked (and has had a grand mal seizure) when he hasn't. Only with the advent of anesthesia has it been possible to use sham treatment consisting of anesthetizing the patient and administering all other steps of the procedure *except* for shock. (The sham-ECT patient is then told, when he or she wakes up, that shock was applied, when it wasn't.)

---

50 See the list of references given at the end of this Appendix.

The sham ECT technique, as currently implemented, can hardly be considered a faithful "placebo," however, since it fails to replicate other aspects of the bonafide treatment, such as anterograde and retrograde amnesia, headache, fatigue, and muscle ache. A valid comparison with ECT would require a placebo that induces injury, which is obviously unethical. But because sham ECT produces none of the typical cognitive or somatic effects of "the real thing," patients are very likely to guess correctly whether they've been shocked or not. Hence, blind breakage is a serious concern even in properly designed studies, and can be expected to result in lower sham ECT response rates than might otherwise be observed.

Nine meta-analyses have compared ECT and sham ECT for depression (Gabor & Laszlo, 2005; Greenhalgh et al., 2005; Janicak et al., 1985: Kho et al., 2003; Pagnin et al., 2004; Ross, 2006; Tharyan & Adams, 2005; UK ECT Review Group, 2003; van der Wurff et al., 2003; see the list of references at the end of this appendix). All except one (Ross, 2006) make the claim that ECT is superior to sham ECT during the treatment period (usually one month), but *none found evidence of any difference in outcome beyond the treatment period.* Claims for the superiority of ECT versus placebo are based on effects seen during the *treatment period* (one month); after the first month, there are no differences between ECT and sham ECT groups. As one author (Ross, 2006) said: "Claims in textbooks and review articles that ECT is effective are not consistent with the published data."

Of the six studies considered by Janicak et al. (1985), only two were said to have produced significant differences between ECT and sham ECT. One was a crossover-design study that gave ECT to the sham group during the treatment period, confounding the results. Another was a very old study (Ulett et al., 1956) in which ECT and "photoshock" results (from a flashing-light technique, combined with hexazol) were conflated. Janicak's review was found by Ross (2006) to contain numerous serious factual errors, calling into question its usefulness.

The UK ECT Review Group (2003) meta-analysis reported that only one study met their inclusion criteria for follow-up studies, and that study found no significant difference. But the study in question had not, in fact, reported any followup data.

The 170-page report by Greenhalgh *et al.* (2005) concluded "there is little evidence of the long-term efficacy of ECT" and that, even in the short-term, "low-dose unilateral ECT is no more effective than sham ECT." The review found "no randomised evidence of the effectiveness of ECT in specific subgroups, including older people, children and adolescents, people with catatonia and women with postpartum exacerbations of depression or schizophrenia."

One of the nine meta-analyses mentioned above, a Cochrane Systematic Review, focused specifically on the effectiveness of ECT for the "depressed elderly" (van der Wurff *et al.*, 2003). This review found no evidence of ECT being effective beyond the treatment period. It identified only one study comparing ECT and sham ECT (O'Leary *et al.*, 1994). The study in question was a re-analysis of data from a paper by three of the reviewers (Gregory *et al.*, 1985), which the reviewers described as having "major methodological shortcomings." The conclusion was that "None of the objectives of this review could be adequately tested because of the lack of firm, randomised evidence."

In addition to meta-analyses of ECT versus sham ECT for depression, there have been meta-analyses along these lines for schizophrenia. A 2001 report by the American Psychiatric Association admits that none of five pre-1980 ECT versus sham ECT studies found any differences in outcomes, even in the short term, but claimed that three more recent studies demonstrated "a substantial advantage" for ECT (Abraham & Kulhara, 1987; Brandon *et al.* 1985; Taylor & Fleminger, 1980). In all three studies, however, both patient groups were receiving antipsychotic medications, and any advantage for ECT was, in fact, short-lived. In the Leicester ECT Trial (Brandon et al. 1985), for example, both the ECT and the sham ECT groups improved on all four measures used. "Global psychopathology" did not differ at all. However, the authors note: "The superiority of real ECT was not demonstrated at the 12- and 28-week follow-up." Another of these studies (Taylor & Fleminger, 1980) found that during treatment there was equal improvement in both groups, although ECT improved general psychopathology faster than sham ECT for the first four weeks (only). In the Taylor & Fleminger (1980) study, the psychiatrists (unblinded) were the only ones to perceive any difference in the groups. Nurses and relatives did not see a difference. This might be because psychiatrists are better trained to rate symptoms, but it is also likely reflective of researcher bias, since most ECT studies are done by researchers who strongly advocate the use of ECT and believe in its benefits.

A more recent study (Sarita *et al.*, 1998) of 36 people diagnosed with schizophrenia found no differences in double-blind ratings on four symptom measures after one, two, three, or four weeks of treatment, in a comparison of sham ECT with either bilateral or unilateral ECT.

A Nigerian study (Ukpong *et al.*, 2002), likewise, failed to find significant differences between ECT and sham ECT at the end of treatment. It also failed to find differences 20 weeks later.

A 2005 update of the Cochrane database (Tharyan & Adams, 2005) found a short-term advantage for ECT over sham ECT, but "no evidence that this early advantage for ECT is maintained over the medium to long term." The Cochrane reviewers found that even in the short term, ECT was less effective than antipsychotic medication.

More recently, Poublon & Haagh (2011) published a systematic review of ECT for schizophrenia, drawing only on randomized, controlled studies that included a sham ECT arm. They found six such studies. In four of the six, ECT produced statistically significant improvement relative to sham ECT, during the treatment period, but in followup, no significant differences remained. The authors said: "No evidence was found proving the superiority of ECT over sham-ECT after followup."

On the whole, ECT effectiveness is not far different from sham ECT (and *no* different, after the treatment period), raising the possibility that it is the anesthesia, rather than the electrical shock, that produces much of the therapeutic effect. Tending to confirm this possibility is the fact that ketamine, a general anesthetic, has recently been found to be therapeutic, on its own, for treatment of severe depression (McGirr *et al.*, 2014). If a study were to compare anesthetics used in ECT with respect to the effect on depression outcomes, analysis of variance might reveal the extent to which choice of anesthetic influences outcomes, and this would tend to establish the degree to which therapeutic effect is due strictly to anesthesia. Unfortunately, no such studies have yet been done.

It's often claimed that ECT prevents suicide. But there are no suicide studies comparing ECT and sham ECT, and the existing literature fails to support the contention that ECT is protective against suicide.

Read and Bentall (2010) looked at 13 studies comparing suicide rates of groups who have and have not had ECT (see Table II of their paper). Only 2 out of 13 studies claimed a significant suicide-protective effect for ECT; one study dates to 1945, the other to 1948 (hence both date to the era of "unmodified" ECT—ECT without anesthesia). Ironically, in one of these studies (Ziskind *et al.*, 1945), two patients died during ECT. In the other study, 80 people with "manic-depressive psychosis" (who never got ECT) were compared with 74 similarly diagnosed individuals treated with ECT (Huston & Locher, 1948). Six patients (7.5%) of the untreated group and one patient (1.4%) of the treated group killed themselves during a follow up period of between three and seven years. It is impossible to determine whether the different suicide rates can be attributed to ECT, however, because the untreated individuals were more disturbed than the treated group: Twice as many (31% v 16%) were classified as having "severe illness," and more (72% v 58%) came from disturbed families ("mental illness," alcoholism, criminality, etc.). But also, significantly, more patients in the untreated group (52% v 34%) were men. It's well known that men have a three-fold higher suicide rate than women.

In their decidedly pro-ECT book, Shorter and Healy (2007), cite five studies to support their claim that ECT prevents suicide. One study is mistakenly cited twice with different authors, namely the 1945 study by Ziskind *et al.*, reporting on chemically induced seizures (using the GABA inhibitor Metrazol). So the actual number of ECT studies is four—but since the Ziskind study conflates ECT data with Metrazol-seizure data, there really are just three. One of the three studies is the 1948 paper by Huston & Locher, already discussed above. Also cited are papers by Avery & Winokur (1976) and NIMH (Kellner *et al.*, 2005). The 1976 Avery study recorded deaths among 519 depressed patients three years post-discharge. There were four suicides among the 257 who had received ECT (1.6%) and four (1.5%) among the 262 who had not—hardly a convincing show of ECT's suicide-prevention capabilities. The NIMH study, meanwhile, was not a study of suicide. It was a study of *suicidal ideation*. It provided no data on suicide rates.

There remains no definitive evidence that ECT prevents suicide. Most of the "evidence" on this subject (e.g., Huston & Locher, 1948) comes from an era when ECT was not available as an outpatient procedure. In other words, it comes from the days of mental institutions, when patients were either in confinement (and thus *prevented* from committing suicide) or under intensive medical observation, in conditions that would make suicide much harder to achieve.

On the other hand, there is considerable evidence that ECT itself kills people.

Textbooks and consent forms claim that the risk of death from ECT is very small. The American Psychiatric Association (2001) has said (citing no references) "Published estimates from large and diverse patient series over several decades report up to 4 deaths per 100,000 treatments." APA gives a "reasonable current estimate" of the risk as (at most) 1-in-10,000, which is the number quoted in many consent forms. This is far from an accurate estimate.

Frank (1978) reviewed 28 articles in which psychiatrists had reported ECT-related deaths. Of 130,216 ECT patients, there were 90 ECT-related deaths, or one death per 1,447 people, seven times greater than the official APA claim.

Impastato (1957) reported 254 deaths caused by ECT and calculated a mortality rate of one per 1,000 patients overall, with a death rate in people over age 60 of 1-in-200—*fifty times* higher than the American Psychiatric Association estimate.

At the Mayo Clinic in Minnesota, 18 out of 2,279 ECT patients died within 30 days of treatment (Nuttall *et al.*, 2004). The paper reporting this result claimed "all deaths appear to be unrelated to ECT," despite six being "of unknown cause" and two being from heart attack or stroke (outcomes known to be associated with ECT). Eight additional patients died within two weeks, of "cardiac events." What makes these results especially hard to explain is that ECT is usually not administered to anyone who isn't in good physical health; and in this case, recipients had the advantage of being in the care of Mayo Clinic, one of the top health-care providers in the world.

In a 1980 survey of British psychiatrists involving ECT–related deaths that occurred during or within 72 hours of treatment, there were four reported deaths in 2,594 patients (Pippard & Ellam, 1981). That's a rate of one per 648.5 people—15 times greater than the American Psychiatric Association claim. Of the additional six people who died within a few weeks of ECT, two were from heart attacks and one from stroke (common causes of death from ECT). With these three deaths included, the rate becomes one death per 371 ECT patients.

In a Norwegian survey, 3 out of 893 women—1 in 298—died as a result of ECT (Strensrud, 1958).

Freeman and Kendell (1980) attempted to survey 183 patients who had received ECT in 1976, to determine their attitudes toward ECT treatment. However, 22 patients were either dead or "could not be traced." Twelve were definitely dead; four had killed themselves. If we count only the two deaths that occurred during ECT, the mortality rate comes to 1 in every 92 patients.

All of these findings show much higher mortality among ECT patients than has been claimed by APA. Consent forms do not cite data showing the true rate of death to be far greater than the 1-in-10,000 claimed by APA. Therefore, patients who consent to ECT are hardly doing so in an informed manner.

The APA's sample information sheet (representing suggested wording for informing patients abut ECT) includes the following language:

> During ECT, a small amount of electrical current
> is sent to the brain. This current induces a
> seizure that affects the entire brain, including
> the parts that control mood, appetite, and sleep.
> ECT is believed to correct biochemical
> abnormalities that underlie severe depressive
> illness. We know that ECT works . . .

The phrase "a small amount of electrical current" is misleading, because the amount of current involved (typically 0.9 amps at 450 volts) is known to be fatal if applied to other parts of the body. Likewise, the statement "ECT is believed to correct biochemical abnormalities" is blatantly fraudulent, since there is no consensus view on how ECT achieves its effects. Indeed, the consensus view is that ECT's mechanism of action is not understood.

When consent is granted based on this kind of misinformation, it cannot be considered "informed consent." Also, when consent forms fail to mention that there is no difference in outcome, after one month, in patients who receive sham ECT versus real ECT (except for fewer side effects with sham), patients are seriously misled.

Adverse cognitive effects are well known to be associated with

ECT, and this is another area in which patients are under-informed. In spite of repeated claims (for 50 years) that ECT is safe, the first large-scale prospective study of cognitive outcomes following ECT did not occur until 2007, when outspoken ECT advocate Harold Sackeim, *et al.* (2007) found that autobiographical memory was significantly (p < .0001) worse in patients both immediately after ECT and six months later. At both time points, the degree of impairment was significantly correlated to the number of shocks, with women and older patients particularly impaired. Impairment was also greater among those who received bilateral ECT rather than unilateral ECT, prompting Sackeim to conclude "there appears to be little justification for the continued first-line use of bilateral ECT in the treatment of major depression." (Despite this, bilateral ECT remains the most common form of ECT in use today.)

A 1980 study (Freeman *et al.*, 1980) produced the longest followup data to date. ECT patients performed worse than non-recipients on ability to recall famous personalities from the 1960s and also on personal memories from early childhood; the average time since ECT was *8.4 years.* Most people would consider this permanent memory damage.

In addition to significant retrograde amnesia, there are reports of ECT resulting in anterograde amnesia (the inability to retain newly learned information; a learning disability). The American Psychiatric Association report (2001) cites 11 studies demonstrating anterograde amnesia in the first few weeks after ECT, concluding that during this time, "returning to work, making important financial or personal decisions, or driving may need to be restricted." Nevertheless, the APA report states "no study has documented anterograde amnesia effects of ECT for more than a few weeks," which is blatantly false. Feliu *et al.* (2008) found that anterograde amnesia persists for four weeks. Two studies (Porter *et al.*, 2008; Squire & Slater, 1983) showed that anterograde memory is degraded for at least two months. Halliday *et al.* (1968) demonstrated anterograde memory deficits lasting three months.

For many years, it has been claimed that ECT produces no brain damage. And yet, in the 1940s it was commonly accepted that ECT owes its effects to brain damage. In 1941, Walter Freeman, in a paper called "Brain-damaging therapeutics," wrote: "The greater the damage, the more likely the remission of psychotic symptoms. [...] Maybe it will be shown that a mentally ill patient can think more clearly and more constructively with less brain in actual operation" (Freeman, 1941). A review in the *Lancet* (Alpers, 1946) described ECT-induced hemorrhages and concluded that "all parts of the brain are vulnerable—the cerebral hemispheres, the cerebellum, third ventricle and hypothalamus." In two memory tests used to assess brain damage, Goldman *et al.* (1972) found that ECT patients scored worse than a non-ECT control group at both 10 and 15 years after ECT, which "suggests that ECT causes irreversible brain damage."

According to Read and Bentall (2010), "In the 1940s and 1950s autopsies consistently provided evidence of brain damage, including necrosis (cell death)."

In a review of the first twenty years of autopsies, Allen (1959) concluded: "damage to the brain, sometimes reversible but often irreversible, occurred in the course of electric shock treatments."

CT scans have demonstrated frontal lobe atrophy among ECT patients (Calloway *et al.*, 1981; UK ECT Review Group, 2003). One review acknowledged that "both anterograde and retrograde memory impairment are common" (Rami-Gonzalez *et al.*, 2001). The same review documented various forms of neurobiological dysfunction underlying the subtypes of ECT-induced memory dysfunction: Retrograde amnesia was found (not surprisingly) to be a consequence of electrochemical dysfunction of the limbic-diencephalic subcortical areas involved in information retrieval; while in anterograde amnesia, the medial temporal lobe is most affected.

The medical literature thus strongly suggests that ECT causes brain damage, which is the only reasonable way to explain the persistent and

146

often irreversible cognitive deficits that occur in patients who have been repeatedly shocked. But again, consent forms leave out this important information, throwing into question the notion that *any* ECT patient has ever truly given "informed" consent.

John Read and Richard Bentall, in their review of the literature (Read & Bentall, 2010), observed: "The continued use of ECT . . . represents a failure to introduce the ideals of evidence-based medicine into psychiatry. This failure has occurred not only in the design and execution of research, but also in the translation of research findings into clinical practice." Their conclusion was that "the cost-benefit analysis for ECT is so poor that its use cannot be scientifically justified." On this basis, and because consent forms do not accurately portray the risks of electroconvulsive therapy, continued use of ECT in a therapeutic setting can only be considered unethical.

References for this Appendix

Abraham, K. & Kulhara P. (1987). The efficacy of ECT in the treatment of schizophrenia. *British Journal of Psychiatry* 15, 152-155.

Allen, I. (1959). Cerebral lesions from ECT. *New Zealand Medical Journal* 58, 369-377.

Alpers B. (1946). The brain changes associated with electrical shock treatment: A critical review. *Lancet* 66, 363-369.

American Psychiatric Association (2001). *The Practice of Electroconvulsive Therapy Recommendations for Treatment, Training and Privileging. A Task Force Report of the American Psychiatric Association*, 2nd ed. APA: Washington, DC.

Avery, D. & Winokur, G. (1978). Suicide, attempted suicide, and relapse rates in depression. *Archives of General Psychiatry* 35, 749-753.

Blease, C.R. (2013), Electroconvulsive therapy, the placebo effect and informed consent. *Journal of Medical Ethics.* 2013 Mar;39(3):166-70

Brandon, S., Cowley, P., McDonald, C., Neville P., Palmer, R. & Wellstood-Eason, S. (1985). Leicester ECT trial: Results in schizophrenia. *British Journal of Psychiatry* 146, 177-183.

Calloway, S., Dolan, R., Jacoby, R. & Levy, R. (1981). ECT and cerebral atrophy. *Acta Psychiatrica Scandinavica* 64, 442-445.

Feliu, M., Edwards, C., Sudhakar, S., McDougald, C., Raynor, R. & Johnson, S. (2008). Neuropsychological effects and attitudes in patients following ECT. *Neuropsychiatric Disease and Treatment* 4, 613-617.

Frank, L.R. (1978). *The History of Shock Treatment.* Frank: San Francisco. ISBN-13: 978-0960137619.

Freeman, C. & Kendell, R. (1980). E.C.T, Patients' experiences and attitudes. *British Journal of Psychiatry* 137, 8-16.

Freeman, W. (1941). Brain-damaging therapeutics. *Diseases of the Nervous System* 2, 83.

Gabor, G. & Laszio, T. (2005). The efficacy of ECT treatment in depression: A meta-analysis. *Psychiatria Hungarica* 20, 195-200.

Goldman, H., Gomer, F. & Templer, D. (1972). Long-term effects of ECT upon memory and perceptual motor performance. *Journal of Clinical Psychology* 28, 32-34.

Greenhalgh, J., Knight, C., Hind, D., Beverley, C. & Walters, S. (2005). Clinical and cost-effectiveness of electroconvulsive therapy for depressive illness, schizophrenia, catatonia and mania: Systematic reviews and economic modelling studies. *Health Technology Assessment* 9, 1-170.

Gregory, S., Shawcross, C. & Gill, D. (1985). The Nottingham ECT study. *British Journal of Psychiatry* 146, 520-524.

Halliday, A., Davison, K., Browne, M. & Kreeger, L. (1968). A comparison of the effects on depression of bilateral and unilateral ECT to the dominant and non-dominant hemispheres. *British Journal of Psychiatry* 114, 997-1012.

Huston, P.E. & Locher, L.W. (1948). Manic-depressive psychosis. Course when treated and untreated with electric shock. *Archives of Neurology and Psychiatry* 60, :37-48.

Impastato, D. (1957). Prevention of fatalities in ECT. *Diseases of the Nervous System* 18, 34-75.

Janicak, P., Davis, J., Gibbons, R., Eriksen, S., Chang, S. & Gallagher, P. (1985). Efficacy of ECT: A meta-analysis. *American Journal of Psychiatry* 142, 297-302.

Kellner C., Fink M., Knapp R., Petrides G., Husain M. & Rummans T. (2005). Relief of expressed suicidal intent by ECT. *American Journal of Psychiatry* 162,977-982.

Kho, K., van Vreewijk, M., Simpson, S. & Zwinderman, A. (2003). A meta-analysis of electroconvulsive therapy in depression. *Journal of ECT* 19, 139-147.

Lagasse, R. (2002). Anesthesia safety, model or myth? A review of the published data and analysis of current original data. *Anesthesiology* 97, 1609-1617.

McGirr, A., Berlim, M.T., Bond, D.J., Fleck, M.P., Yatham, L.N., & Lam, R.W. (2014), A systematic review and meta-analysis of randomized, double-blind, placebo-controlled trials of ketamine in the rapid treatment of major depressive episodes. *Psychol Med.* 2014 Jul 10:1-12.

Nuttall, G., Bowersox, M., Douglas, S., McDonald, J., Rasmussen, L., Decker, P., Oliver, W. & Rasmussen, K. (2004). Morbidity and mortality in the use of electroconvulsive therapy. *Journal of ECT* 20, 237-241.

O'Leary, D., Gill, D., Gregory, S. & Shawcross, C. (1994). The effectiveness of real versus simulated electroconvulsive therapy in depressed elderly patients. *International Journal of Geriatric Psychiatry* 9, 567-571.

Pagnin, D., de Queiroz, V., Pini, S. & Cassano, G. (2004). Efficacy of ECT in depression: A meta-analytic review. *Journal of ECT* 20, 13-20.

Pippard, J. & Ellam, L. (1981). *Electroconvulsive Treatment in Great Britain, 1980: A Report to the Royal College of Psychiatrists.* Gaskell: London. ISBN 9780902241077.

Poublon, N.A. & Haagh, M. (2011). The efficacy of ECT in the treatment of schizophrenia. A systematic review. Erasmus Journal of Medicine, 2:1, 16-19.

Porter, R., Heenan, H. & Reeves, J. (2008). Early effects of ECT on cognitive function. *Journal of ECT* 24, 35-39.

Rami-Gonzalez, L., Bernardo, M., Boget, T., Salamero, M., Gil-Verona, J. & Junque, C. (2001). Subtypes of memory dysfunction associated with ECT: Characteristics and neurobiological bases. *Journal of ECT* 17, 129-135.

Read, J. and Bentall, R. (2010), "The effectiveness of electroconvulsive therapy: A literature review," *Epidemiologia e Psichiatria Sociale*, 19, 4, 333-347.

Ross, C. (2006). The sham ECT literature: Implications for consent to ECT. Ethical Human *Psychology and Psychiatry* 8, 17-28.

Sackeim, H., Prudic, J., Fuller, R., Keilp, J., Lavori, P. & Olfson, M. (2007). The cognitive effects of ECT in community settings. *Neuropyschophamacology* 32, 244-254.

Sackett, D., Rosenberg, W., Gray, J., Haynes, R. & Richardson, S. (1996). Evidence based medicine: What it is and what it isn't. *British Medical Journal* 312, 71-72.

Sarita, E., Janakiramiaiah, N., Gangadhar, B., Subbakrishna, D. & Rao, K. (1998). Efficacy of combined ECT after two weeks of neuroleptics in schizophrenia. *NIMHANS Journal* 16, 243-251.

Shorter, E. & Healey, D. (2007). *Shock Therapy: A History of ECT in Mental Illness.* Rutgers University Press: New Jersey.

Squire, L., Slater, P. & Miller, P. (1981). Retrograde amnesia and bilateral electroconvulsive therapy: Long-term follow-up. *Archives of General Psychiatry* 38, 89-95.

Strensrud, P. (1958). Cerebral complications following 24,562 convulsion treatments in 893 patients. *Acta Psychiatrica Neurologica Scandinavica* 33, 115-126.

Taylor, P. & Fleminger, J. (1980). ECT for schizophrenia. *Lancet* 315:8183, 1380–1383.

Tharyan, P. & Adams, C. (2005). Electroconvulsive therapy for schizophrenia. *Cochrane Database of Systematic Reviews* Issue 2, CD000076.

UK ECT Review Group (Carney, S., *et al.*) (2003). Efficacy and safety of ECT in depressive disorders. *Lancet* 361, 799-808.

Ulett, G., Smith, K. & Gleser, G. (1956). Evaluation of convulsive and subconvulsive shock therapies utilizing a control group. *American Journal of Psychiatry* 112, 795-802.

Ukpong, D., Makanjuola, R. & Morakinyo, O. (2002). A controlled trial of modified electroconvulsive therapy in schizophrenia in a Nigerian teaching hospital. *West African Journal of Medicine* 21, 237-240.

Van der Wurff, F., Stek, M., Hooogendijk, W. & Beekman, A. (2003). Electroconvulsive therapy for the depressed elderly. *Cochrane Database of Systematic Reviews* Issue 2, CD003593.

Ziskind, E., Somerfeld-Ziskind, E. & Ziskind, L. (1945). Metrazol and electroconvulsive therapy of the affective psychoses. *AMA Archives of Neurology and Psychiatry* 53, 212-217.

Index

KAS THOMAS has written widely on science and technical topics for *BigThink.com* and his own blog at http://asserttrue.blogspot.com (which has had over five million visits in 7 years). He holds degrees in biology and microbiology from the University of California (Irvine and Davis campuses, respectively) and is a former Regents' Fellow. Thomas is also the author of the mental-illness memoir *Of Two Minds* (ISBN 1507753926).

Visit **hackyourdepression.com**. Sign up for our mailing list (privacy assured).